Getting Started:
Reculturing Schools to Become Professional Learning Communities

Robert Eaker
Richard DuFour
Rebecca DuFour

National Educational Service
Bloomington, Indiana

Cover design by Grannan Graphic Design, Ltd.
Text design by T.G. Design Group

Printed in the United States of America

Printed on recycled paper

ISBN 1-879639-89-0

Dedication

This book is dedicated to my wife, Star, and my children, Robin and Carrie, and in memory of my parents, Raymond and Jewell Eaker. Appreciation also is extended to Jerry and Elner Bellon for their many years of encouragement, support, and friendship.

—Robert Eaker

I dedicate this book to my co-authors, Becky and Bob, each of whom has enriched my life both personally and professionally.

—Richard DuFour

To Hannah and Rick, and to all those who dedicate themselves to helping others make their dreams come true.

—Rebecca DuFour

Table of Contents

About the Authors

Robert Eaker, Ed.D., is the executive vice-president and provost at Middle Tennessee State University and a former fellow with the National Center for Effective Schools Research and Development. Dr. Eaker has written widely on the issues of effective teaching, effective schools, helping teachers use research findings, and high expectations and student achievement. Drs. Eaker and DuFour coauthored *Creating the New American School* (National Educational Service, 1992) and *Professional Learning Communities at Work* (National Educational Service, 1998). Dr. Eaker has spoken at numerous national meetings, such as the National Association of Secondary School Principals, and the Association for Supervision and Curriculum Development. Dr. Eaker was chosen by Phi Delta Kappa for the "People in Educational Evaluation and Research" interview series that appeared in the October 1986 issue of *Phi Delta Kappan.* He regularly consults with school districts throughout the nation on school improvement issues.

Richard DuFour, Ed.D., is the superintendent of Adlai Stevenson High School District 125 in Lincolnshire, Illinois. During his tenure Stevenson High School has become one of the most recognized and celebrated high schools in America. He has received his state's highest award as both a principal and a superintendent. He was presented the "Distinguished Alumni Award" of Illinois State University and was named as one of the nation's "Top 100" school administrators by *Executive Educator* magazine.

Dr. DuFour has helped to develop a video series on the principalship for the Association of Supervision and Curriculum Development and is a featured columnist for the *Journal of Staff Development.* He has authored four books and more than 50 professional articles and has consulted for professional organizations, state departments of education, and school districts throughout the United States and Canada.

Rebecca DuFour, M.Ed., currently serves as the principal of Boones Mill Elementary School in Boones Mill, Virginia. She has 15 years of experience in public schools as a teacher and an administrator at both the building and central office levels. Ms. DuFour graduated from the University of Virginia with a Master's degree in Educational Leadership and Policy Studies. She is also a graduate of National Staff Development Council's Academy X.

Ms. DuFour is one of the featured principals in the Video Journal series entitled "Effective Leadership in an Era of High Standards." She has presented on the PLC model of school improvement in numerous states and in Canada and will be a featured presenter at National Educational Service's PLC institutes in Chicago, San Diego, and Houston.

Foreword

A Commitment to School Improvement

T he National Educational Service (NES) began its relationship with Richard DuFour and Robert Eaker over a decade ago with the publication of Richard DuFour's book *The Principal as Staff Developer*, edited by Dennis Sparks, Executive Director of the National Staff Development Council. The follow-up book, *Creating the New American School,* by Richard DuFour and Robert Eaker, was published in 1992, marking the beginning of what has become a truly great relationship for the NES with two of our country's greatest practitioners.

Rick and Bob's life work evolved into the publication of *Professional Learning Communities at Work: Best Practices for Enhancing Student Achievement* in 1998. Even in its draft form, the book was immediately recognized by the Association for Supervision and Curriculum Development (ASCD) as a resource of extreme value. ASCD partnered with the NES for the first printing of the resource; their logo is still printed on the title page of the book. *Professional Learning Communities at Work* continues to be one of ASCD's most prominent resource offerings.

In the spring of 1998, the NES held the first conference on Professional Learning Communities in Chicago, where over 500 attendees were introduced to the model. This conference was followed by our first Professional Learning Communities Summer Institute, held in Tremblant, Quebec, Canada. The demand from schools and districts for more information on the Professional Learning Communities model continued to grow at an astonishing rate. This hunger for information was the driving force behind the NES' development of the video series of the same name, which was released in August of 1999. This three-part staff development video and facilitator's guide has been used in thousands of schools across the country and continues to be in high demand.

Interest and participation in the PLC Summer Institute continued to grow, and in 1999, the NES moved the Institute's location from Tremblant to Hilton Head, South Carolina. In 2000, it moved to the Lincolnshire Marriott and Adlai Stevenson High School in Lincolnshire, Illinois. The move to Lincolnshire provided the opportunity to highlight not only the program, but also the facilities at Adlai Stevenson High School that have evolved from the proven success of implementing a professional learning community. Current demand for the PLC Summer Institute created the need for two locations in 2002—Lincolnshire, IL, and San Diego, California—with a fall conference being held in Houston, Texas. Other states are seeking the opportunity to host Institutes in 2003 and beyond, broadening even further the NES' ability to reach educators throughout the country.

At the 2001 Summer Institute, the NES offered attendees a videotape of the keynote presentations by Bob Eaker, Rick

DuFour, and Becky DuFour. Requests for the videotapes and the transcripts from these three keynotes were overwhelming. Many attendees also requested transcripts of the Question and Answer Panel Discussion held at the conclusion of the Institute. In response to the demand for the transcripts and a comprehensive overview of the Professional Learning Communities model, we worked with Bob, Rick, and Becky to develop this book, *Getting Started: Reculturing Schools to Become Professional Learning Communities.* I am more than confident that you will find this an outstanding tool to use as you move down the continuum of becoming a professional learning community.

The NES is very proud to be the home of one of this nation's greatest school improvement models—Professional Learning Communities. Through our books, video series, conferences, summer institutes, and by providing professional development in the Professional Learning Communities model, we are able to assist tens of thousands of professional educators in defining and realizing their goals. By partnering with Rick, Bob, and Becky, we feel we truly can make a difference in the lives of educators and students. Rick, Bob, and Becky are not only our partners and our colleagues, but they are also our friends. We couldn't ask to be associated with three finer human beings and representatives of the education profession.

—Jeffrey C. Jones
Publisher and President
National Educational Service

Getting Started:
A Conceptual Framework for Creating
A Professional Learning Community

With the 1998 publication of *Professional Learning Communities at Work: Best Practices for Enhancing Student Achievement,* we presented the premise that the most promising strategy for substantive school improvement is developing the capacity of school personnel to function as a professional learning community (PLC). We were able to strengthen that argument by citing the consensus of leading researchers from within and outside of education who agreed that the characteristics of a professional learning community are essential to the sustained improvement of any organization. Our book illustrated the principles of a PLC at work in the real world of schools and offered strategies and tools to assist educators in making the transition to a PLC.

We have now worked with school districts, state departments of education, and professional organizations throughout the United States and Canada to assist in the implementation of the PLC concepts. The response has been overwhelmingly positive. The ideas that drive the PLC model strike a chord with educators. It typically requires very little to persuade them that students and teachers alike would benefit if schools operated as learning communities.

The enthusiastic response to the PLC model often has been tempered, however, by the uncertainty of educators regarding their ability to create a learning community within their own settings. They question whether or not their schools or school districts have the resources, competencies, leadership, or will to work through the challenges inherent in the cultural transformation of a school. While embracing the abstract idea of the PLC model, they lack confidence in their ability to move from abstraction to implementation, from promise to reality in their own settings. Thus, it is common for participants in our workshops to seek the step-by-step recipe they can follow to create a PLC in their own school.

The bad news, of course, is that no such recipe exists. Neither quick fixes nor fool-proof formulas are available to those interested in the PLC model. The structural and cultural changes required to advance a traditional school on the continuum of becoming a PLC are inherently non-linear and complex. Progress is typically incremental, characterized more by starts and stops, messiness, and redundancy than sequential efficiency.

But while those interested in the PLC model do not have access to a fool-proof recipe, a solid conceptual framework is available to guide their efforts. The elements of this framework illustrate how schools operate when they are functioning as PLCs. Schools that keep the framework at the forefront as they engage in the improvement process have a model by which they can assess the effectiveness of their efforts.

The PLC conceptual framework can be grouped into three major themes that are evident in the policies, programs, and practices of the school or district. The themes are: (1) a solid foundation consisting of collaboratively developed and widely shared mission, vision, values, and goals, (2) collaborative teams that work interdependently to achieve common goals, and (3) a focus on results as evidenced by a commitment to continuous improvement.

Laying the Foundation of a PLC: Shared Mission, Vision, Values, and Goals

A school cannot function as a PLC until its staff has grappled with the questions that provide direction both for the school as an organization and the individuals within it. What is our purpose, the core reason our organization was created? What must we become as a school to better fulfill that purpose? What collective commitments must we make to move our school in the direction we want it to go? What targets and timelines are we willing to establish to serve as benchmarks of our progress? When a staff can develop consensus on their collective responses to these questions, they are articulating the shared mission, vision, values, and goals that constitute the foundation of a PLC. These essential building blocks then become the basis for all of the decisions that drive the school.

Imagine a school that functions as a professional learning community resting on a four-legged table with one leg representing mission, another leg vision, the third leg values, and the final leg goals. Each leg presents a question for the school to consider. The mission or purpose leg focuses on the question: *"Why do we exist?"* It challenges each member of the group to clarify the fundamental purpose of the school. The vision leg asks the question: *"What kind of school or district do we hope to become?"* The group is called upon to articulate a realistic, credible, desirable future that is so compelling they will be motivated to work together to make that future a reality. The values leg asks, *"How must we behave in order to create the kind of school we hope to become?"* This leg represents the essential ABCs of school improvement as it challenges the people within the organization to specify the <u>a</u>ttitudes, <u>b</u>ehaviors, and collective <u>c</u>ommitments they will demonstrate in order to advance the school toward their vision. The fourth leg, the goals leg, addresses the question: *"What steps are we going to take and when will we take them?"* The goals leg challenges school personnel to transform the good intentions of their vision statement into specific targets to be achieved at different stages of the improvement process.

If the school is to withstand the inherent turmoil involved in substantive change, its foundation must be solid. Each of the four legs must be firmly in place. If a leg is missing, if it is not anchored in the table, or if it is too short, the school's future improvement efforts are likely to be built on a very shaky base that is almost certain to topple at the first sign of pressure. When schools are inattentive to mission, vision, values, and goals; when they address the topics superficially instead of embedding them in their cultures; or when they short-change the process just to complete the task, the core foundation of their improvement initiatives is unlikely to withstand the inevitable stresses that will accompany their efforts. The first critical rule of building a learning community is to build a solid foundation of shared mission, vision, values, and goals.

Developing High-Performing, Collaborative Teams

Schools that function as professional learning communities are **always** characterized by a collaborative culture. Teacher isolation is replaced with collaborative processes that are deeply embedded into the daily life of the school. Members of a PLC are not "invited" to work with colleagues: they are called upon to be contributing members of a collective effort to improve the school's capacity to help all students learn at high levels.

The driving engine of the collaborative culture of a PLC is the team. All members of the staff are assigned to one or more teams that are called upon to work interdependently to achieve one or more common goals. Individual teachers give up a degree of personal autonomy in exchange for collective authority to answer the most critical questions of teaching and learning. Teams work together to clarify the intended outcomes of each grade level, course, or unit of instruction. They develop common assessments that they consider valid measures of student mastery. They jointly analyze student achievement data, draw conclusions, and establish team improvement goals. They support one another and share strategies and materials as they work together to accomplish goals that they could not achieve by working alone. The teams have the benefit of time, focus, parameters, access to information, and ongoing support as they engage in collective inquiry and action research. They work together in an ongoing effort to discover best practices and to expand their professional expertise.

Developing a Results-Oriented Culture

What is the basis for determining what works best? For a professional learning community the answer is clear—student learning. In more traditional schools there is often an emphasis on how much staff or students "like" a particular approach or initiative. In a professional learning community, however, attempts at school improvement are judged on the basis of how student learning is affected. Thus, teachers in a PLC move beyond the pious affirmation, "We believe all students can learn" found in the mission statements of schools around the world. The focus on results forces them to delve deeper and to grapple with the questions that drive a PLC. Individually and collectively they ask: "If we truly believe all kids can learn, what is it that we want them to learn? How can we be certain all students have learned it? How can we respond to assist those students who are not mastering the intended outcomes?"

Getting Started

If the PLC model offers only a conceptual framework for transforming a school rather than a prescribed recipe, those interested in creating a PLC in their own school are still left with the question, "Where do we begin?" The examples and stories that follow are intended to help answer that question. The following chapter focuses on the cultural shifts that must take place as schools move from more traditional ways of doing things to functioning as a professional learning community. Chapter 2 addresses the issue of finding the time to do all the things that are required to transform a school into a professional learning community. It explains how one elementary school principal determined important priorities in her school and in her principalship. Chapter 3 presents the lessons learned from one school that made the transition to becoming a professional learning community in one year with dramatic results. Chapter 4 recognizes that readers of this book will still have many questions. We have tried to anticipate some of these questions by engaging in a conversation focusing on the major issues associated with getting started. Chapter 5 urges readers not to wait on others. Even though conditions may not be ideal, it is essential to get started—to do what you can do. The last sections—Artifacts and Case Studies—contain examples, handouts, and case studies intended to serve as useful tools to help move the PLC process forward in a school or district.

It is important to understand, however, that no school has ever made progress toward becoming a PLC until some of its members took steps to make it happen. There is a natural tendency to wait for someone else to take the initiative to improve our schools. Superintendents wait for more enlightened boards of education or more favorable state legislation, principals look to the central office, department chairpersons look to the principal, teachers look to department chairpersons, and so on.

It is a common occurrence at the conclusion of our workshops for a participant to approach us and express the hope that someone else in the organization will act on the information we presented. Those participants have missed the point. It is certainly preferable for people throughout the organization, particularly key leaders, to commit to the PLC initiative. In fact, we have concluded that the elements of a PLC offer no substitute for weak and ineffective leadership. Nevertheless, we have seen individuals at all levels of a school district serve as a catalyst for moving a school forward on the PLC continuum. Principals have helped create PLCs in their schools despite indifference from the central office. Department chairpersons have been successful in helping their departments function as a learning community in a school that does not. Individual teachers have banded together to demonstrate the power of a collaborative team in schools where most teachers continue to work in isolation. We caution the readers of this book to avoid the tendency to wait for someone else to advance the PLC model in their schools, and challenge them instead to identify and take personal steps to make it happen.

Finally, perhaps a word or two about the style of the book is appropriate. Readers who are familiar with our previous works will find this book much more informal. We made a conscious decision to write this book in a more conversational style in which we share our personal experiences with readers.

Improving schools in significant and meaningful ways is an incremental, complex process that requires among other things, patience, passion, and persistence. An important element of the process involves learning from each other. In part, reculturing involves sharing what we know with each other. We are constantly searching for ideas, processes, and products that can help schools function as professional learning communities. We hope this book is a significant contribution to this process of sharing.

Chapter 1

Cultural Shifts: Transforming Schools Into Professional Learning Communities

Robert Eaker

Professional learning communities are our best hope for reculturing schools. A common belief is that changing the structures of schools—how they are organized—is the primary way to change behavior. But changing the structure of schools is not enough. Changing the structure without altering the belief system will not produce fundamental changes. Seymore Sarason (1996) observes,

> if you want to change and improve the climate and outcomes of schooling—both for students and teachers, there are features of the school culture that have to be changed, and if they are not changed, your well-intentioned efforts will be defeated. (p. 340)

If we think of "school culture" as involving, at least in part, "how we do things around here," then we need to consider two key questions:

1. How are things done in a professional learning community as opposed to more traditional schools?

2. What cultural shifts need to occur if traditional schools are to become professional learning communities?

Changing the school culture so that it becomes a professional learning community involves many elements:

- Collaboration

- Developing mission, vision, values, and goals

- Focusing on learning

- Leadership

- Focused school improvement plans

- Celebration

- Persistence

Collaboration

As we think about reculturing schools, here is an excellent place to start: We must shift from a culture of teacher isolation to a culture of deep and meaningful collaboration (Table 1.1).

Table 1.1
Cultural Shift: Collaboration

Traditional Schools	Professional Learning Communities
• Teacher Isolation	• Collaborative Teams

Traditional schools are characterized, to a great degree, by teacher isolation. It has been said that the traditional school often functions as a collection of independent contractors united by a common parking lot. Here, then, is a fundamental shift: professional learning communities strive to create a culture of collaboration. Collaboration by invitation will not work. It is never enough. This is a key point. In a professional learning community, collaboration is **embedded** into every aspect of the school culture. Every major decision related to the learning mission is made through collaborative processes.

But just how does this collaborative culture work in a professional learning community? Here are some fundamental assumptions we make about collaboration:

- If schools are to improve, staff must develop the capacity to function as professional learning communities.

- If schools are to function as professional learning communities, they must develop a collaborative culture.

- If schools are to develop a collaborative culture, they must overcome a tradition of teacher isolation.

- If schools are to overcome their tradition of teacher isolation, teachers must learn to work in effective, high-performing teams.

The culture of a professional learning community is characterized, in part, by collaborative teams whose members work interdependently to achieve common goals. Special attention must be paid to the "interdependence" and "common goals" if we are going to have high-quality collaboration and truly effective teams.

Our work with collaborative cultures has led us to believe that there are several important keys to highly effective teams:

- Collaboration is embedded in routine practices.

- Time for collaboration is built into the school day and school calendar.

- Products of collaboration are made explicit.

- Team norms guide collaboration.

- Teams pursue specific and measurable performance goals.

- Teams focus on key questions associated with learning.

- Teams have access to relevant information.

These keys can also serve as an assessment instrument to determine how teams work in your school.

Mission

The second major cultural shift involves the school mission. Clearly and unequivocally, the fundamental mission of a school that functions as a professional learning community is learning. Table 1.2 shows the cultural shift involved when a professional learning community develops a mission statement.

Most schools have addressed the issue of their "mission" in some way. Unfortunately, in traditional schools, the mission seldom goes beyond some pleasant affirmation about "each and every child" becoming a "lifelong learner," etc. In a professional learning community the mission statement is given meaning by addressing three corollary questions. If we believe the primary mission of schools is learning, then:

1. What do we expect students to learn?

2. How will we know what students have learned?

3. How will we respond to students who aren't learning?

Table 1.2
Cultural Shift: Developing a Mission Statement

Traditional Schools	Professional Learning Communities
1. Statements are generic.	1. Statements clarify what students will learn.
2. Statements are brief, such as "We believe all children can learn."	2. Statements address the question, "How will we know what students are learning?"
	3. Statements clarify how the school will respond when students do not learn.

Addressing these three fundamental questions positions the school to move from a culture that has a primary emphasis on "teaching" to a culture with a primary emphasis on "learning."

Vision

Once we have addressed the issues related to the mission, we can devote our attention to developing a shared vision that is meaningful, credible and, most important, used. Table 1.3 shows the cultural shift involved when a professional learning community develops a vision statement.

Notice the differences. In a traditional school, a committee is usually charged with developing a vision statement. Typically, the committee meets a number of times and a consensus of opinions begins to emerge. Ultimately, a document is drafted that essentially reflects the results of "averaging" opinions.

Table 1.3
Cultural Shift: Developing a Vision Statement

Traditional Schools	Professional Learning Communities
1. Statements are average opinions.	1. Statements are research-based.
2. Statements deteriorate into wish lists.	2. Statements are credible and focus on essentials.
3. Statements are often ignored.	3. Statements are used as a blueprint for improvement.
4. Statements are often dictated or developed by few.	4. Statements are widely shared through broad collaboration.

In a professional learning community, the collaborative process takes an entirely different approach. We begin developing the vision statement by seeking out and learning about "best practices." For example, we study the research on effective schools or the latest research on assessment or parent involvement. In other words, rather than the vision statement being the result of collective opinions, a professional learning community develops a vision statement based on collective inquiry.

Writing a vision statement often deteriorates into writing a "wish" list: "We have to have more technology, new physical education equipment, new band uniforms, etc." But in a professional learning community, we reflect on our learning mission and ask ourselves, "What are the essentials? If we did an excellent job with the essentials, what would the results look like?" In other words, we describe the school or school district we are seeking to become by describing how excellent programs would look. We can only do this if we are rather definitive in our vision statement.

Perhaps the biggest difference between a traditional school and a professional learning community regarding the vision statement is the fact that in many schools the vision statement is generally ignored. In a professional learning community, the vision statement forms the basis for school improvement planning, budgeting, and staff development, among other activities. Discussions and decisions should inevitably focus on the question, "How will this help us move the school toward the vision we have for our school?"

Values

The next cultural shift that must occur if we are to become a professional learning community is in the area of shared values or commitments. Table 1.4 shows the cultural shift involved when a professional learning community develops value statements.

All schools operate from a set of values. However, in most schools these values are seldom the result of a collaborative dialogue. Instead, they tend to be rather random and seldom discussed. In a professional learning community, collaborative processes are developed in order to articulate the commitments that we will need to make together if we are going to become the kind of school we described in our vision statement. Perhaps the biggest cultural shift that must occur in the area of values is the shift from belief to behavior.

In traditional schools, the focus is on "beliefs." We see documents where each major point or sentence begins with the

Table 1.4
Cultural Shift: Developing Value Statements

Traditional Schools	Professional Learning Communities
1. Values are random.	1. Values are linked to vision.
2. Statements are excessive in number.	2. Statements are few in number.
3. Values are articulated as beliefs.	3. Statements are used as a blueprint for improvement.
4. Statements focus on self.	4. Values are articulated as behaviors and commitments.

words "we believe." A professional learning community recognizes that beliefs are important, but also makes an effort to go beyond beliefs and focus on behaviors. We ask, "How do we need to behave if we are going to become the kind of school we said we seek to become?" As a result, each of the statements in the values document of a professional learning community should begin with the words "we will."

Traditional schools do a good job of describing how other groups should behave. Thus, discussions about shared values and commitments often lead to commitments that others need to make if the school is to excel. In a professional learning community, the focus is on ourselves. We are frequently asked, "How do we write value statements that address all of the various areas associated with schooling?" The answer is this: each group—teachers, administrators, students, parents, support personnel, etc.—writes value statements for their group.

Goals

Of course, we recognize that the value or commitment statements are not enough. We have to develop plans. We have to ask, "What steps are we going to take and when are we going to take them?" Collaboratively developing goals is not a new or novel activity for educators. Table 1.5 compares the way goals

Table 1.5
Cultural Shift: Developing Goal Statements

Traditional Schools	Professional Learning Communities
1. Statements are random.	1. Statements are linked to vision.
2. Goals are excessive in number.	2. Goals are few in number.
3. Goals focus on means rather than ends.	3. Goals focus on desired outcome.
4. Goals are impossible to assess or measure.	4. Goals are translated into measurable performance standards.
5. Goals are not monitored.	5. Goals are monitored continuously.
	6. Goals are designed to produce short-term wins and also stretch aspirations.

are written in a traditional school to goal development in a professional learning community.

In a professional learning community, goals, like value statements, are tied directly back to the vision we have for the school. Professional learning communities do not have an excessive number of goals. In more traditional schools, goals frequently focus on the "means" rather than the "ends." There is a focus on activities and tasks to be accomplished. A professional learning community focuses on the desired outcomes and asks, "Why is this a goal? What are we trying to accomplish?"

Goals developed by a professional learning community are also translated into measurable performance standards and are monitored continuously. When developing goals, the learning community ensures that some goals will produce short-term successes and a few goals will stretch their aspirations.

Focus on Learning

One of the most important cultural shifts that must take place if schools are to perform as professional learning communities involves a shift from a primary focus on **teaching** to placing the primary focus on **learning** (Table 1.6). Obviously, high-quality teaching is of critical importance, so what does it mean to shift the primary focus from teaching to learning? The main difference

Table 1.6
Cultural Shift: Focus on Learning

Traditional Schools	Professional Learning Communities
• Primarily focus on teaching	• Primarily focus on learning

is in the questions we ask. A professional learning community has deep collaborative discussions about the key questions that are associated with learning, including the following:

- What exactly do we expect students to learn?
- How will we know what students are learning?
- How can we assist and support students in their learning?
- Based on a collaborative analysis of the results of our efforts, what can we do to improve student learning?
- How can we recognize and celebrate improvements in student learning?

These are just a few of the kinds of questions that collaborative teams of teachers address in schools that function as professional learning communities.

Curriculum. Naturally, a focus on learning will involve extensive discussions about the curriculum. While all schools focus on curriculum issues, there are major differences between traditional schools and schools that function as professional learning communities. Table 1.7 highlights these differences.

In addition to aspects of the curriculum that have previously been discussed, there is a concerted effort to reduce content. In a professional learning community, time is viewed as a precious resource, so attempts are made to focus our efforts on less, but more meaningful content. The time that is saved allows the teaching of more meaningful content at a greater depth.

Best practices. Teachers in professional learning communities are constantly seeking out "best practices." This is done through the process of collective inquiry. In traditional schools, decisions about improvement strategies are made by "averaging

Table 1.7
Cultural Shift: Curriculum

Traditional Schools	Professional Learning Communities
1. Each teacher independently decides what to teach.	1. Collaboratively agreed upon curriculum focuses on what students are expected to learn.
2. Curriculum overload is common.	2. Reduced content means meaningful content is taught at greater depth.
	3. Assessment is developed through collaboration.
	4. A plan for responding to students who are not learning is developed through collaboration.

opinions." In professional learning communities, decisions are research-based with collaborative teams of teachers seeking out "best practices."

Where do collaborative teams of teachers look for best practices? The answer is anywhere and everywhere! They read and discuss books and professional journals. They search the Internet. They attend conferences and workshops. They belong to professional associations. And they visit other schools that are having outstanding success. This quest for "best practices"— collective inquiry—is one of the most fundamental cultural

Table 1.8
Cultural Shift: Collective Inquiry

Traditional Schools	Professional Learning Communities
• Decisions about improvement strategies are made by "averaging opinions."	• Decisions are research-based with collaborative teams of teachers seeking out "best practices."

shifts that occurs as schools become professional learning communities (Table 1.8).

Culture of research and results. These collaborative teams of teachers are rather skeptical. They recognize that while things may work well in one school it does not necessarily mean they will work equally well in another school.

The essence of this cultural shift is that collaborative teams of teachers are building a culture of experimentation by engaging in active research. They are not content to accept the "external" validation of researchers. They want practices to be "internally" validated in their school, in their classrooms, with their students. Table 1.9 highlights this difference.

Here is an important aspect of this cultural change: More traditional schools tend to make decisions based primarily on how well teachers "like" particular approaches. (A professional learning community recognizes that feelings are important, but makes the primary basis for embedding particular practices into the school culture the effect that these practices have on student learning.) This emphasis on how practices affect learning helps to create a results-oriented culture.

Table 1.9
Cultural Shift: Research and Results

Traditional Schools	Professional Learning Communities
1. Effectiveness of improvement strategies is externally validated. Teachers rely on others outside the school to identify what works.	1. Approaches are internally validated. Teams of teachers try various approaches and collaborate on how the approaches affect student learning.
2. Emphasis is placed on how teachers like various approaches.	2. The effect on student learning is the primary basis for assessing various improvement strategies.

Leadership

Much has been written about the critical role leadership plays in a professional learning community. One of the most fundamental cultural shifts that takes place as schools become professional learning communities involves how teachers are viewed. In traditional schools, administrators are viewed as being in leadership positions, while teachers are viewed as "implementors" or followers. In professional learning communities, administrators are viewed as leaders of leaders. Teachers are viewed as transformational leaders (Table 1.10).

Frequently, we hear a superintendent remark that the "leadership team" attended a retreat or workshop. More than likely, the superintendent is referring to administrators when

Table 1.10
Cultural Shift: Leadership

Traditional Schools	Professional Learning Communities
• Administrators are viewed as being in leadership positions while teachers are viewed as "implementors" or followers.	• Administrators are viewed as leaders of leaders. Teachers are viewed as transformational leaders.

speaking about the "leadership" team. Obviously, administrators hold important leadership positions, but in a professional learning community the view of leadership is extended to include teachers. In fact, teachers are viewed as holding the key leadership positions in a school.

Think of it this way. Transformational leadership implies that effective leaders change the lives of those around them. They motivate and inspire. They get those with whom they work to accomplish things that seem impossible. If the central purpose of schools is learning, who is in the best position to transform students' lives, motivate and inspire students, and get students to do things they never thought they could do? The answer is clear—teachers! In fact, when we think of the best teachers we ever had, we often use adjectives such as "caring," "encouraging," "challenging," and "motivating" to describe them. It is interesting that these adjectives are often the same adjectives we use to describe the characteristics we would hope to find in an effective leader.

Focused School Improvement Plans

If the primary mission of a professional learning community is learning and if we are committed to improving learning in our school, then we need plans for getting from point A to point B. In professional learning communities, the school improvement plan is viewed as the primary vehicle for sustained, cyclical, continuous school improvement. Table 1.11 shows the cultural shift involved when a professional learning community develops focused school improvement plans.

Table 1.11
Cultural Shift: School Improvement Plans

Traditional Schools	Professional Learning Communities
1. School improvement plans focus on a wide variety of things.	1. School improvement plans focus on a few important goals that will affect student learning.
2. The goal is often to "get the plan turned in." Then the plan is ignored.	2. The school improvement plan is the vehicle for organized, sustained school improvement.

Many, if not most, states require some form of school improvement planning. However, in some schools the culture is such that the goal of the school improvement planning process is "to get the thing turned in!" In a professional learning community the process of collaboratively developing yearly school improvement plans reflects a culture that values continuous improvement.

In a professional learning community, the school improvement plan focuses on a few key goals that will have a significant impact on learning. In more traditional schools, the focus of the school improvement plan is often on managerial issues such as changing the school schedule or calendar or committee structure. A key question that should be asked about any school improvement plan is this: "If all of the goals in the plan are accomplished, what will be the impact on student achievement?"

Celebration

What is celebrated in schools? What rituals and ceremonies are in place to reinforce what is valued? In professional learning communities, there is a conscious effort to use the power of celebration to promote the values the school professes to hold dear. Table 1.12 describes the cultural shift involved when a professional learning community celebrates its achievements.

Virtually all schools have ceremonies and celebrations. In traditional schools, celebrations and recognition are rather infrequent and often focus on things other than the central mission of the school. (What is the first thing one sees when entering many high schools? An athletic trophy case.) When recognizing teachers, traditional schools almost always recognize groups of teachers rather than individuals. There is a reluctance to publicly recognize and praise individuals. It is just the opposite in a professional learning community. Celebration is frequent, tied directly to the school's values, and recognizes the accomplishments of individuals as well as groups.

Professional learning communities develop ceremonies to recognize and celebrate improvement, in addition to recognizing

Table 1.12
Cultural Shift: Celebration

Traditional Schools	Professional Learning Communities
1. Celebration is infrequent. When teachers are recognized, the celebration almost always focuses on groups.	1. School improvement plans focus on a few, important goals that will affect student learning.
2. Celebration and recognition occur when students reach an arbitrary standard.	2. In addition to celebration and recognition when a standard is met, celebrations recognize improvement.
3. Recognition is limited to a few individuals.	3. The school works hard to "create" winners and celebrate their successes.
	4. Celebrations are linked to the vision and values of the school and improved student achievement.

students who have met a high arbitrary standard. Think of it this way: traditional schools set arbitrary standards in order to recognize the highest-achieving students. The Principal's List, BETA Club, National Honor Society, and selection as senior class valedictorian are examples of this. Is this a good thing? Yes! We want to celebrate and recognize the accomplishments of our top academic students. But here is the problem: in more traditional schools, a relatively small percentage of students think they have a chance of ever being recognized in these ways. A professional learning community recognizes its highest achievers and also develops plans to recognize and celebrate improvements that other students are making. If we say we value improvement in student achievement, then we should celebrate it when it occurs.

Persistence

Location, location, location. It is often said that these are the three most important words in real estate. Using this analogy, the three most important words in a professional learning community might well be persistence, persistence, persistence! In traditional schools, improvement efforts frequently shift as new fads or trends come along. In professional learning communities, a conscious effort is made to make sure we "stay the course" and avoid jumping on to the next fad that comes along. The school is committed to "staying the course" in the attainment of the school vision. New initiatives are only implemented if it is determined that the change will help the school achieve its vision of the future. The leader's role in a professional learning community is to promote, protect, and defend the school's vision and values and to confront behavior that is inconsistent with the school's vision and values (Table 1.13).

In our presentations, we have frequently pointed out that some superintendents and principals view their districts and schools as Christmas trees. Improvement is analogous to decorating the tree. They think of the various education fads as ornaments and the key to having a good district or school is to get as many ornaments as you can on the tree. Of course, leaders of professional learning communities also encourage experimentation, but it is the *context* in which experimentation

Table 1.13
Cultural Shift: Persistence

Traditional Schools	Professional Learning Communities
1. Improvement efforts frequently shift as new fads or trends come along.	1. The school is committed to "staying the course" in the attainment of the school vision. New initiatives are only implemented if it is determined that the change will help the school achieve its vision of the future.
	2. The leader's role is to promote, protect and defend the school's vision and values and to confront behavior that is incongruent with the school's vision and values.

occurs that is different from their more traditional counter-parts. In a professional learning community, the school vision is the anchor to which all experimentation is tied. One of the most frequently asked questions in a professional learning community is this: "Will this (change, initiative, program, etc.) move us toward the vision we have for our school?" We do not try something new simply because it is the latest idea. We try it because we believe it may help us achieve our vision of what we want to become.

Teachers often have the view, "This too shall pass." Unfortunately, this has often been the case based on their past experiences. In a professional learning community, teachers can take comfort in the fact that school administrators are committed to becoming the kind of school described in the vision statement. The leader's job in a professional learning community is not "decorating the tree." Instead, his or her task is to embed the characteristics of professional learning communities in the school culture and then promote, protect, and defend them. Most importantly, the leader must be willing to confront behavior that is incongruent with the values that the groups have collaboratively agreed upon. Linking this willingness to confront incongruent behavior with celebrations of the best examples of the school's values when they occur is a powerful way to communicate that we intend to stay the course. These efforts go a long way toward incrementally reculturing your school.

A Nonlinear Process

One last note: Making these cultural shifts is difficult and nonlinear (that is, it is not a step-by-step process). Some of these cultural shifts will occur fairly quickly, while others will take years. When and how these shifts occur will ultimately depend on the quality of leadership and collaboration that is present. You do not need to look outside of your school for the keys to making these cultural shifts. Remember, what you need to reculture your school lies within. Collaborate with one another. Support one another. Care for one another. Encourage one another, and remarkable things will happen.

Chapter 2

Time, Perspective, and Priorities

Richard DuFour

It has been said that humans are story-seeking animals. The cultures, religions, and big ideas of ages past have been transmitted from one generation to another through parables, fables, and legends. I will share several stories with you to illustrate how a professional learning community works in the real world.

"Where do I find the time?"

The first story occurred at a workshop where I was presenting. During a break, a principal came up to me and asked, "How do you expect me to find the time to do all this professional learning community stuff with all the other demands I have on my job? By the time I finish all the 'have to's,' the things I must do as part of my job, I don't have time to build a professional learning community."

I had some sympathy for what he said. The issue he presented is a common one. In essence, he was saying, "I don't have the time to improve my school when I'm so busy managing it." I believe that, although the list of "have to's" may be daunting, a person can always find the time to do the "must do's." Moving the professional learning community effort to the "must do" list is the first step in transforming a school.

Another story will illustrate the principal's point. Imagine an empty glass pitcher, the kind you would fill with lemonade and ice on a hot summer day. This empty pitcher represents time, which is fixed and constant. There are only so many hours in the day and so many days in the week. You cannot create more time, just as you cannot make the pitcher bigger.

Now imagine a large bag of rice. The many grains of rice represent all of the "have to's" that demanded his time. To understand what these demands do to the principal's time, we pour the rice into the empty pitcher. The pitcher is now over half full. It certainly is heavier than it used to be, and for good reason. The rice represents a very demanding list of "have to's." The principal has to administer the contracts, evaluate teachers, attend staff meetings, discipline students, attend administrative meetings at the district office, fill out state reports, address the concerns of parents, manage the busses and budgets . . . the list goes on and on.

Let's add one more prop to this story: three tennis balls. Imagine these bright yellow balls represent the big ideas of a professional learning community. If we try to put them in the pitcher after we have poured in all of the rice representing the principal's "have to's," there is no room left for the tennis balls. As the principal insisted, there really is not enough time.

Finding a New Perspective

What is the solution to this dilemma? We cannot give this principal more time, because time is fixed. We could suggest he try delegating some of those "have to's" to other people in the organization to free some of his time. In fact, I suggested this alternative, but he insisted that everything he did was absolutely essential and could not be entrusted to others. He was very determined to have me agree that he simply did not have time to improve his school.

Instead, I advised him that the issue at hand was not one of time, but rather one of perspective. What he needed to do was change his perspective about the nature and essence of his job. As Peter Drucker (1992) has observed, the way in which a person defines his or her job will determine to a large extent the way in which he or she does that job.

Perspective is a powerful thing. Consider the story of a woman who observed three tradesmen at work. Each of the tradesmen was doing the same activity. When she asked the first tradesman what he was doing, he answered, "I'm just laying brick." When she asked the second tradesman the same question, he answered, "I'm building a wall." When she asked the third tradesman, he answered, "I am building a cathedral." Each one had the same task to complete, but three very different perspectives on what he was accomplishing.

The proper perspective for someone who is trying to start a professional learning community is best illustrated by the true story of an elementary school principal in a rural county that has very few resources. The per pupil expenditures in her county rank it in the bottom 10% of the state. They have very few resources to devote to education. Furthermore, she has no assistant in a school of 450 students. She has a very limited clerical staff. She begins each day at 5:30 a.m. by taking the phone calls from teachers who will not be reporting to work. She has to find substitute teachers, deal with the discipline problems first thing in the morning when the kids get off the bus, evaluate teachers, and attend meetings. In other words, she has all the same "have to's" that the other principal did, and more; yet, she was able to build a professional learning community in her school in a very short time. How did she do that? Did she have more time? No. Did she have fewer responsibilities? No. She had all the same "have to's," but she approached her job from a different perspective. Instead of focusing on "laying brick," she chose to focus on "building a cathedral."

First Things First

Leading organizational theorists provide insights on how effective leaders manage their time. Stephen Covey (1989) contends that "the essence of the best thinking in the area of time management can be captured in a single phrase: organize and execute priorities" (p. 49). The admonition that leaders should do first things first and second things not at all has become the axiom of effective management (Drucker, 1992).

The principal in this story was able to build a professional learning community because she focused on first things first. By sharing her story, I will illustrate the four main priorities for leaders when they build professional learning communities:

1. Focus on learning.

2. Focus on collaborative culture.

3. Focus on results.

4. Provide timely, relevant information.

PLC Priority One: Focus on Learning

From the time she joined the school as the principal, this principal made it clear that the very fundamental purpose of the school was **learning**. She and her staff went beyond the traditional writing of a mission statement typically done in schools. Instead, they reviewed the impact of the school's practices, programs, and procedures on learning. The principal's skillful use of critical questions ultimately led her staff to address the issues that drive learning communities.

The first question she posed was simple: "Our mission statement says we are committed to learning for all students. If that is true, exactly what is it we want each child to learn—by grade level and by unit of instruction?" She asked her staff to do more than pool opinions as they attempted to answer the question. She provided them with state curriculum standards, district curriculum guides, curriculum recommendations from a number of professional organizations, and teacher's editions of a variety of textbooks. She also helped them analyze the strengths and weaknesses of their students on state and national assessments from the previous year. She asked them to identify skills students would be expected to demonstrate on the state test that were not being covered adequately in the school's curriculum. In other words, she helped them gain shared knowledge on the best thinking regarding curriculum and the current levels of student achievement **before** she asked them to specify what each student should know and be able to do in each unit of instruction, subject, and grade level.

She then asked her staff to identify areas of the existing curriculum that might be eliminated to provide more time for focusing on the essential outcomes they had identified.

Together, she and her staff addressed one of the fundamental challenges a school must face as it becomes a learning community—eliminating inessential curriculum. A consensus gradually emerged on what was essential, and the inessential content was eliminated. Every teacher in every course became clear on the answers to the question, "What is it we want students to know and be able to do?"

Next, the principal asked the staff to answer the second critical question of professional learning communities: "Now that we are clear on what students should learn, how do we know if they have learned it?" The teachers began to develop common assessments for each grade level. After the staff agreed that focusing on average scores was inappropriate for a school committed to each student's success, they worked together to specify the standards of performance on each subtest and test that would indicate student mastery of intended outcomes. Since the faculty also hoped to use performance assessments in monitoring student learning, they began to clarify the criteria by which they would judge the quality of student work. Teaching teams worked together to practice applying the criteria until they became very consistent in their assessment of student work. The common assessments and consistent application of rubrics enabled teachers in this school to greatly improve their ability to assess each student's learning on an ongoing basis.

The principal then asked the staff the one question that separates professional learning communities from traditional schools: "How will we respond when students do not learn?" The fact that not all students learn initially is not a surprise. In virtually every school in North America teachers begin the school year teaching to the best of their ability, hoping to help every child learn. Yet, by the third or fourth week of school, it is evident that some students are not understanding the material. Although this happens in every school, every year, the way in which schools respond to the situation varies greatly.

In most schools, students and teachers enter into an unstated contract. If effect, the teacher says:

> Look kids, we have 3 weeks to learn this unit. I cannot give you 4 weeks. We have too much material to cover. We're also limited to 50 minutes on this topic during each school day. I can't make it 55 minutes. The bell will ring and you must go to your next class. So time is constant for each of you—50 minutes per day for 3 weeks—and the level of support you will receive from me is also a constant. I can't give you a lot of individual attention. I have too many students, and it would be unfair to hold back the rest of the class for you.

But when schools hold time and instructional support as constants, what is the resulting variable? Learning. Unit by unit, some students achieve the outcomes and some do not. Most schools are content to allow learning to be the variable, while they hold time and support as constants. But not a learning community. Learning is the only constant in a professional learning community. Staff say, "These are the **essential** outcomes, not the 'nice-to-know' outcomes or the 'here's-a-chance-to-learn-this' outcomes. Because we believe these outcomes are essential and all students can achieve them, we will find ways to provide additional time and support for those students who struggle."

The principal and her faculty began to develop systematic strategies to ensure any student who was having difficulty learning would be given more time and support during the school day. Their strategies for doing this included using grant money to hire a tutor and developing materials—actual teaching guides—that parents could use to reinforce the skills their children were being taught. Making these materials available to parents was a concrete way for the staff to say, "Because we know that you want your children to learn, here are materials you can use at home to help your children learn these essential outcomes."

The principal's efforts continued with the following initiatives:

- She created **business partnerships** and invited businesses to truly make a difference by allowing their employees to work with students one on one.

- She worked with the high school to create **internships** so high school students interested in education as a career could be released from high school a part of each day to help elementary students master skills.

- She created a **peer tutoring system** within the school. Every kindergarten student was assigned to a fifth-grade mentor who tutored his or her kindergarten buddy each week in essential skills.

- She worked with staff to create a **master schedule** that allowed students to receive additional small-group or individualized instruction in ways that did not remove them from their classrooms during direct instruction.

In short, she made certain that every student who needed it would receive additional time and support for learning. Her unwavering focus on learning helped her staff clarify their belief that learning was the first priority of their school.

You should consider the following questions if you are going to build a professional learning community in your school:

1. Does every teacher understand what each student should know and be able to do after completing the unit of instruction, course, and grade level?

2. What systems are in place to monitor each student's learning on a timely basis?

3. What happens when a student is not learning? How does the school respond?

4. What systems are in place to provide these students with additional time and support?

If you are serious about transforming your school into a professional learning community, learning must become its first priority.

When I became a principal I did not understand the importance of focusing on learning. In fact, I was under the impression that as the instructional leader, my responsibility was to focus on instruction. I asked teachers to provide me with detailed course descriptions that clarified what they were going to teach and when they were going to teach it. I would occasionally ask to see their lesson plans to monitor what they were teaching. I used a very elaborate clinical supervision model as part of my process for observing teachers in the classroom. I would conduct pre-observation conferences so teachers could tell me what they were going to teach and how they were going to teach it. During the classroom observation, I would dutifully record what teachers said and did in their classrooms. In the post-observation conference, the teacher and I would study what he or she had said and done in the class I had observed. Then we discussed how the lesson might have been taught differently. I was skilled in clinical supervision, and I spent hours and hours every year in the process. I did not learn my focus was misplaced until later. Instead of asking, "What and how are the teachers teaching?" I should have been asking, "Are the students learning?" This relentless focus on student learning represents the first priority that drives professional learning communities.

PLC Priority Two: Focus on Collaborative Culture

The second priority that drives a professional learning community is the importance of creating a collaborative culture in which staff members work together in interdependent teams that pursue common goals. The challenge facing leaders in this area is not in creating the teams, but rather in providing the focus, time, support, and parameters critical to effective teamwork. The principal in our story was able to meet that challenge by using several strategies.

First, she created team structures that ensured every staff member was a contributing member of a team. Most of her teams were grade-level specific, but teachers also worked as members of interdisciplinary and vertical (multi-grade) teams as well. Next she created a master schedule that gave every collaborative team time once a week and every vertical team time once a month. It is fundamentally unfair to teachers to insist that collaboration is a priority and then fail to provide them with time to collaborate during the school day. Because this principal provided her teachers with time to meet in teams during the school day, it was evident that working together in a collaborative team was a priority in her school.

Her next challenge was to ensure that teachers used this time for collaboration productively. Teachers who have spent most of their lives working in isolation often find it difficult to effectively use their team time when first asked to collaborate. Conversations often drift to topics that have little correlation to student achievement such as how many points should we deduct when students turn in late work, how long will we spend on this unit, or which novel should we ask students to read. The principal in our story helped her teachers focus on issues correlated to student achievement by providing them with 15 critical questions (found on page 146 in the Artifacts section).

As you review the questions, you will find that they fit easily within three general questions:

1. What do we want students to learn?

2. How will we know if they have learned it?

3. What are we going to do if they do not learn it?

Our principal also provided her teams with support to help them through the inevitable rough spots in their work. She asked teams to **develop written protocols or norms** to determine how they would conduct their meetings. These protocols became the commitments each member of the team made to the members of the group to help the team function effectively. Teams were asked to refer to and adhere to the protocols as they conducted their meetings.

The principal attended team meetings on a regular basis and provided feedback and encouragement. She also asked each team to **generate and submit products** they created as a result of answering each of the 15 critical questions. By monitoring the products or artifacts of each team's efforts, she identified the teams that were struggling. She also **created weekly feedback sheets** that help each team provide her with a weekly update on the topics they discussed and the problems they encountered. She provided prompt responses on these feedback sheets to every team every week.

In addition, she asked teams to **develop biannual evaluations** on how they were performing as a team. Twice each year teams were asked to stop and reflect on the following questions:

- Are we being true to our protocols?

- Are we staying focused on the critical questions?

- Are we generating the products we are called upon to create as a team?

- Are we meeting our goals?

The second priority driving this principal's efforts was the need to build a collaborative culture in which teachers worked together to answer important questions of teaching and learning. The following are some of the questions you should ask yourselves as you work to create a professional learning community in your school:

- What is the nature of teams in our school?

- How are these teams organized?

- When do the teams meet?

- Are teams given time for collaboration during the school day?

- Do team conversations focus on questions that will improve student achievement?

- Does the team guide its work by protocols or norms that team members have created and endorsed?

- Are teams asked to assess their effectiveness? If so, on what basis do they make the assessments?

PLC Priority Three: Focus on Results

The third priority that drove the work of our principal was an insistence that school effectiveness should be assessed on the basis of results rather than intentions. She worked with her staff to build shared knowledge on the current reality of their school—its structures, culture, and existing indicators of student achievement. She led them through a consensus-building process to clarify their vision of the school they were working together to create. And she asked every team to establish specific goals to serve as benchmarks of their progress in helping the school achieve better results.

She began this process of building shared knowledge in the summer. She met with every member of the faculty and presented him or her with research articles about the characteristics of schools that are improving. She then discussed these characteristics with each faculty member. She asked questions:

- What are the strengths of our school?

- What are your hopes and dreams for our school?

- What changes would we need to make to realize those dreams?

- How would we know we're making progress?

These conversations became the basis of a shared vision of the school the staff hoped to create. She crafted their individual ideas and hopes into a vision statement and presented it to the faculty early in the year. She invited the faculty to consider and change the statement by making the following comment: "This is what I heard you say. Is this the school year that you envision? Is this the school we should be working toward?"

Once the faculty endorsed the vision statement, the principal led them in analyzing the existing levels of student achievement in their school. Based on their shared understanding of this current reality, the staff decided to focus on two specific, schoolwide improvement goals to move their school closer to their collective vision. Note that the school focused on 2 goals, not 50. They agreed to focus on improving student literacy and math skills as measured on local, state, and national assessments.

In a stroke of genius, our principal helped each grade-level teaching team

- specify the current reality of student achievement in language arts and mathematics for their grade level and

- establish a SMART goal to improve upon that reality.

Schools and teachers typically struggle with goals. They write goals that are impossible to measure, like "Our goal is to help each child become a lifelong learner." While that is a noble goal, we cannot be certain we have achieved it for another 50 years. Or they write goals that focus on activities rather than results, such as "We will integrate technology into the curriculum" or "We will increase the use of cooperative learning by 25%." But in this school, the principal helped each teacher become skilled in writing SMART goals that are:

Strategic and specific

Measurable

Attainable

Results-oriented

Time-bound

For example, the first-grade team found that in the previous year, 65% of first graders earned a score of 3 or higher on the district's reading rubric at the end of the year. They agreed to raise the bar when they set the following SMART goal: "By the end of the 2000-2001 school year, 75% of first graders will score 3 or higher on the district reading rubric." This focus on results helped every team of teachers translate the good intentions of the school vision statement into specific goals which, if realized, would move their school closer to that vision.

Principals who help schools make the transformation to a professional learning community pose the following questions:

- What is the current reality regarding student achievement in our school? (Can we paint a picture of that reality with data? Are the data widely understood by staff? Do we have a clear picture of the school we are attempting to become?)

- Is this vision of the desired future for our school widely shared throughout the staff?

- Have we made commitments regarding what each of us is prepared to do to move the school in the desired direction?

- Have we translated our schoolwide vision into SMART goals for the school?

- Has each team identified the SMART goals it is pursuing to help the school advance toward its vision?

PLC Priority Four: Provide Timely, Relevant Information

From Raw Data to Relevant Information

There is an increasing demand for data-driven schools in this country. I have never felt that schools suffered from a lack of data. Schools and school districts are typically rich with data. The problem has been that the people in the schools are not provided with relevant information that can give them insights into what is and is not working. Data are not information. The fact that someone, somewhere in a district has data on student achievement does not ensure that teachers will be able to use that data to assess their effectiveness or improve their practice.

Several anecdotes from my own experience demonstrate the difference between having data and having information. One time I interviewed a teacher who had applied for a job at Stevenson High School. He had taught physics in Iowa for 20 years, so I asked him to give me some evidence that he had been an effective teacher. This was his answer:

> I have no evidence. I don't know if I have been an effective physics teacher or not. I have no way of knowing whether my kids learned more or less physics than other kids in my school, or other kids in Iowa, or other kids across the nation. Occasionally, a student will come back from college and say my class helped him in college physics, but other than sporadic anecdotal

evidence, I have no way of knowing the degree
of my effectiveness as a teacher.

I do not think this teacher is an aberration. Most teachers,
if they are honest, would give a similar answer: "I have no way
of knowing the degree to which I helped my kids achieve the
essential outcomes of my instruction in comparison to other
students who were trying to achieve those same outcomes."
Although some people say teachers are not interested in data, I
do not find that statement to be true. Teachers are interested in
data if the data are translated into relevant information.

Strategies for Providing Information

The principal in our story was determined to give her teachers timely, relevant, and useful information on the degree to
which their students were learning. Once our principal ensured
that each team understood its specific goals, she focused on providing those teams with timely and relevant information on
their progress. She also provided teachers with the same useful
information that would enable them to determine how their
own students performed in their efforts to meet an agreed-upon
standard, on a valid test, in comparison to other students in the
school attempting to meet that same standard. Her teachers
agreed on the essential outcomes of each unit of instruction and
then developed common assessments specifically outlined with
those outcomes. But they did not just teach, and test, and hope
for the best. They set the bar. They established the performance
level that would indicate mastery for the total test and for each
subtest. So after each of these common assessments, each teacher
could see how his or her students performed compared to the
total group of students who took the test.

A Tale of Two Tests: The ACT and the AP Subject Tests

As a high school principal I observed an interesting phenomenon. Each year, our students and parents would be very anxious about a high stakes test—the ACT exam. Because this exam played a significant role in the college admission process, students and parents looked for every advantage they could find. Parents would enroll their children in private courses on ACT test preparation. This emphasis on scores was reinforced by the area newspapers that compared schools each year on the basis of how students performed on the ACT exam.

Teachers, however, never showed the slightest interest in ACT scores. Ironically, these teachers who were so indifferent to the ACT exam were often intensely interested in the results of another national exam, the Advanced Placement (AP) Exams of the College Board. The teachers of our AP courses became students of the AP exam. They collected old AP exams. They wrote their tests to look like AP exams. They went to conferences so they could talk to other teachers about the AP exam. And they could not wait to get their results! I would receive phone calls all summer from AP teachers who were eager to learn their results. When they finally saw the results, they analyzed every item and every subtest to identify where their students had performed well and where they had experienced difficulty compared to all of the other students in the nation who had taken that test. Most importantly, they then used that information to plan how they would teach the course in the coming year in order to achieve better results.

Why were teachers who were so indifferent to results on the high-stakes ACT exam so impassioned about the results on the lower-stakes AP exam? The AP exam results have four characteristics that make them useful to the teachers of AP courses.

First, the Advanced Placement results **focus on the performance of their own students**. While the ACT exam offers a generic measure of general student achievement in a particular discipline, AP results offer specific information on the performance of specific students.

Second, while the ACT is designed to ensure student scores were distributed along a 36-point scale, AP results report on each student's success **in achieving an agreed-upon standard.** Each student's performance on an AP test is assessed according to a five-point standard. Anyone who scores three or higher is recommended for college credit. The bar is set, and it is theoretically possible for every student taking an AP exam to meet the standard and make it over that bar. The ACT test is designed to ensure that some students will always score in the lowest range, from 1 to 10.

Third, while the ACT was designed as an individual aptitude test, AP exams are specifically designed to assess the degree of student mastery of specific curriculum. Each of these AP exams is a **valid test** because it measures what each student was expected to learn.

Fourth, AP exam results tell each teacher the degree of success of his or her students in meeting the challenging standard of the exam **compared to other students attempting to meet that same standard.** This information helps teachers identify where their students performed well or had difficulty. Teachers can use this feedback to make adjustments in their instructional strategies, pacing, materials, and formative assessments.

This process benefited both students and teachers. Individual students who did not initially pass the exam were given additional time and support until they could demonstrate mastery. And when teachers found that several of their students struggled with a concept, they could solicit support and ideas from their colleagues at their next team meeting.

Members of other professions "practice" their professions. One might hear them say, "I have been practicing law for 15 years," or "I have been practicing medicine for 20 years." But in education, when we talk about the "practice" of teaching, we are referring to the nine weeks or a semester of student teaching where we learned everything we would ever need to know about teaching. In the school of our story, however, teachers have the opportunity to **practice** the art and craft of teaching throughout their careers. They come together every week and engage in professional dialogue on the big questions for teaching and learning, and they help each other develop their skills.

I believe this job-embedded, results-oriented professional dialogue is the very best staff development that a school can provide its teachers. Too often, educators tend to think that staff development is something that happens when we send people away from the school to workshops or college campuses. But the best staff development occurs not in workshops, but in the workplace when teachers come together and learn with and from one another. That is exactly the kind of culture our principal created in her school. She understood that the key to school improvement is people, so she worked with her staff to create conditions that would allow them to grow and learn as part of their routine work practice.

In most schools, we divide teacher working from teacher learning. We say, "our teachers work (that is, they teach) 176 days each school year, and they learn on the 4 teacher institute days." In her school, there was no artificial distinction between working and learning. Teachers came together every week to work together and learn from one another.

The teachers in this school were beneficiaries of the following five rare gifts:

1. A systematic support system to help them with students who were struggling.

2. A clear focus on what students were to learn.

3. Insightful feedback on the performance of their students.

4. Colleagues to help them develop their professional capacity.

5. Time to work with those colleagues.

If only every teacher in every school could receive similar gifts.

Schools that hope to become professional learning communities will focus on the following questions:

- Does every teacher receive timely, relevant feedback on the achievement of his or her students in comparison to other, comparable students attempting to meet the same standard?

- How do teachers use this information?

- Do teachers come together as a team to identify and celebrate strengths in student learning and to identify areas that need additional attention?

- Are teachers working together to support one another in seeking ways to improve individual and team results?

- Does a teacher who may be struggling have someone he or she can talk to, a support system to help him or her grow and learn?

Meeting Unmet Needs

Finally, our principal spoke to the hearts of the people in her school by appealing to their fundamental yearnings, their heartfelt needs. Psychologists tell us that among the most basic of human needs is the **need to feel a sense of personal accomplishment**. This need goes unmet in most schools. Instead, we are assailed by critics who tell us schools are failing, and because we do not focus on results, we have difficulty refuting those critics. In such schools, individual teachers operate in a vacuum, with no basis of comparison and thus no way to assess their personal effectiveness. They can never answer the question, "To what degree am I being successful?"

The teachers in our principal's school can clearly and confidently answer that question. They track their schoolwide goals, and each team can identify its unique contribution to achieving those goals. This focus on individual student mastery has led to a number of success stories. Students who initially struggled to meet standards were given the necessary support to meet the challenge. Individual teachers expanded their repertoire of instructional strategies with the help of their colleagues. Team goals were achieved.

With so much to celebrate in their school, they made celebration a major part of their school life. At every faculty meeting, teams would share a student success, a project the team had accomplished, or the good results they were seeing. Jennifer James (1996) contends that the culture of an organization is found in the stories it tells itself. In our featured school, the principal helped shape the culture of this school by devoting a portion of every faculty meeting to telling stories of success. As a result, the members of the school came to view themselves as successful—individually and collectively.

A second fundamental need we share is the **need to belong**, to feel a sense of "connectedness." This need is also unmet in most schools as teachers work in isolation. Our principal helped break down those walls of isolation. She created a new structure where everyone was asked to be a contributing member of a team, and she gave those teams the resources and parameters they needed to be effective. Ultimately these structural changes shaped the collaborative culture that was essential to the school's becoming a professional learning community.

Finally, we have a deep **need to feel that our life has meaning**, that we are making a difference. According to Victor Frankl (1959), this search for meaning is the primary focus of human life. In fact, the most common reason people choose education as a career is their belief it will give them the opportunity to make a difference. But too often educators lose that belief. Students might not respond to our efforts. Schools and districts may respond to us with what seems like bureaucratic indifference. We can be overwhelmed with the problems and challenges we face, losing faith in our individual ability to make a difference and ultimately becoming numb and jaded.

To meet this need of her staff, our principal constantly appealed to a sense of deep moral purpose within her staff. She made heroes of her teachers, celebrated their efforts, and constantly reminded them that the ultimate purpose of their individual and collective efforts was to make a difference in the lives of their students. She acknowledged their frustration and fatigue, but she did not fall victim to the "woe-is-us mentality" that has come to characterize so many schools. She consistently portrayed the profession as a wonderful and noble calling, the very best work for those who hope to make a positive difference in the lives of others.

This appeal to the staff to fulfill a moral purpose by serving others would probably have sounded pretty hollow if she did not also model that commitment to service. In the last week of her first school year as principal, her entire staff sent a letter to the superintendent thanking him for providing them with such a wonderful leader. They wrote:

> Her personality and leadership style can be summed up in a phrase that we hear often from her: "What can I do to help?" She is constantly looking for ways to make our job easier, which we feel enables us to spend more quality time on instructional issues. Not only is her care for her teachers evident, but her love for and interest in children is obvious. She continually repeats how we need to decide issues based on "what is best for the children."

Service Leadership

What can I do to help? What is best for the children? When these are the questions that drive a leader, we see "servant leadership" at work. Robert Greenleaf made a compelling case for the need for "servant leaders" in *Servant As Leader* (1982):

The servant leader is servant first. It begins with the natural feeling that one wants to serve, to serve first…. The best test of the servant leader, and the most difficult to administer is: "Do those served grow as persons? Do they become healthier, wiser, freer, more autonomous, more likely themselves to become servants?

The principal in our story embodies this idea of servant leadership. She was driven by the question, "What can I do to help teachers develop their full potential as professionals so that collectively we can be more effective in meeting the needs of our children?" By helping her staff grow and learn, she helped them expand their capacity to make a difference in the lives of their students.

The Results Are in for This PLC Success Story

We have been told that professional learning communities are results oriented, so what is the bottom line? What evidence can we present that all of the effort to build a professional learning community produced better results? The district traditionally tracked 12 different indicators of student achievement. At the end of the year, the staff learned that students had tied the school record on one of those 12 areas, but they had established new records in the 11 others. This rural school with few resources, a school that spent in the bottom 10% of the state in terms of per pupil expenditure, scored among the top 6% of the schools on the state achievement test. For its efforts and achievement, the school was presented the Governor's Award for high-performing schools.

Did the principal in this story have more time than the principal who complained he did not have time to build a professional learning community? Not at all. Remember, she had no assistant principal and minimal clerical staff. She had to begin each day at 5:30 a.m. by finding substitute teachers, and she was required to wait in her office each day until 5:00 p.m. until all the buses had finished their routes. She was solely responsible for evaluating every staff member, administering discipline to 450 students, developing the school's budget, and so on. She had all the same "have to's" as the other principal. Furthermore, she was a single mother with huge demands on her time both personally and professionally. It was not easy. She was occasionally frustrated and frequently fatigued. Yet she was able to find the time to persevere because she never stopped focusing on the big ideas, the important priorities of a professional learning community, even while tending to the "have to's" of her position.

The difference between the principal who complained he had no time and the principal who found the time was not in the tasks they had to complete, but in the way in which they approached their tasks. Our principal tended to the "have to's," but she never considered them her primary responsibility. She knew that the very essence of her job was to create conditions that would help staff develop their individual and collective capacity to make a difference in the lives of kids.

This is your life and your career. How do you want to spend it? Managing your building or creating a professional learning community? Laying bricks or building a cathedral? You cannot choose to create more time, but you can choose your focus. Choose well.

Chapter 3

Lessons Learned:
Boones Mill Elementary School

Rebecca DuFour

I first learned about professional learning communities when I was making the transition from being an assistant principal to becoming a principal in Franklin County, Virginia. To prepare for that transition, I attended a leadership conference at the College of William and Mary. The first speaker was Mike Schmoker, an educational consultant and the author of *Results* (1996), who spoke about strategies for helping schools and teachers become more goal-oriented. I felt very affirmed by much of what he said. His message was consistent with the Effective Schools Correlates that the county superintendent had instilled in our schools, and Schmoker's message confirmed many of the things we were already doing in the Franklin County Public Schools.

The next presenter was Rick DuFour. He described schools that focused on learning rather than teaching as schools that

- were united by a shared vision, collective commitments, and common goals;

- involved teachers in collaborative teams that considered the important questions of teaching and learning;

- integrated continuous improvement processes into their regular practices; and

- focused on results.

I was tremendously excited by the model he described. I felt it offered the exact conceptual framework for where I hoped to take my new school.

When I returned to my school division, I shared the information on learning communities and gave my supervisor a copy of Rick DuFour and Bob Eaker's book *Professional Learning Communities at Work* (1998). He was also enthusiastic about the PLC model, so we organized study teams of the administrators in our school division to discuss the book. Later that year, a cadre of the division's administrative team attended a full-day conference on professional learning communities.

I had already begun my responsibilities as a principal during this time of studying and learning, but the truth was, what I was learning had not yet affected my practice as a principal. I was very timid about implementing the ideas. I convinced myself I needed more time to learn before implementing any of the good ideas I had heard. I realize now that I was simply making excuses instead of exploring the steps I could take to introduce the elements of a professional learning community into my school.

At the end of the school year, I left Franklin County to work in the central office of another district. I soon found, however, that I missed the children, teachers, and energy of an elementary school, so I returned to Franklin County to be the principal of Boones Mill Elementary School. My year in the central office had helped me understand that effective principals do not just study how to improve their schools. They also take steps to act on what they have learned. When I accepted the position at Boones Mill, I promised myself I would do everything I could to help the staff build a professional learning community. This chapter provides many of the specific steps we took to implement the strategies, concepts, and assumptions that support a professional learning community.

Honoring the History and Finding Common Ground

I took my first step in beginning to build a relationship with the faculty before I assumed the position as principal. I asked the former principal for 45 minutes with the faculty on the last day of school. During that time, I asked each staff member to do three things:

1. Celebrate an achievement from the school year.

2. Share how they planned to use some of their personal time in the summer.

3. Confer with the teachers at their grade level or staff with similar job responsibilities to schedule a time to meet with me during the summer.

In July I met with all staff members in small groups and asked each group to consider and answer three questions:

1. What makes this school so great?

2. What do I as the principal need to know about this school?

3. What steps can we take together to make this an even better school?

The staff members spoke openly about their feelings and hopes while I listened intently, recorded everything they said in a notebook, and occasionally nodded to acknowledge their ideas and feelings.

These discussions helped me understand the current reality of the school, at least as it was perceived by the staff. The responses I received were very consistent. When asked to identify what made the school so good, every person, without fail, said it was the people of the school: the children, the families, and most importantly, the staff. Nobody said, "We have a really great computer lab" or "a brand new reading textbook." As Bob and Rick suggest, a school's culture and people, not its equipment or materials, determine the quality of the school. My staff knew this instinctively.

Answers to the second question that asked what I needed to know about the school provided me with a sense of the school's history. I wanted them to not only share key information with me, but I also wanted to hear their versions of the story of Boones Mill. As Bob and Rick note, the culture of a school is found in the stories it tells itself.

Answers to the third question on how the school could become even better helped us begin to build a shared vision upon common hopes. By the end of the summer, every stakeholder in the building had offered his or her ideas about what would take us to a better future.

During August I looked for the common themes that emerged from our summer dialogues, and I shared those themes with the faculty during the first week of school. I never said, "We're going to build our shared vision this summer," but that is exactly what we were doing. In his presentations, Rick will often talk about the importance of speaking to the hearts of people—addressing not only what they do, but also what they feel—if we are hoping to change the culture in a school. During our dialogues, the staff spoke from their hearts because they were in small groups conducive to discussion and because they were comfortable with the people with whom they were sharing.

Creating a Guiding Coalition

Our next effort was to devise a conceptual framework to guide us as we began to take steps toward our vision. The staff was already familiar with the Effective Schools correlates, and they had studied the Basic Schools model. During the summer and fall, I shared with them the vocabulary and concepts of a professional learning community. Their welcome back letter from me included not only their class lists and a draft copy of the schedule but also several articles Rick had written on professional learning communities for the *Journal of Staff Development* (1997a; 1997b; 1997c). In this and other times in which I introduced PLC vocabulary and concepts, we built a common vocabulary and shared new ideas without me ever pronouncing, "We're going to build a professional learning community." I did not want the staff to believe their new principal was going to come in and change everything.

When the PLC concept was finally introduced to the faculty as a model of school improvement, the introduction came not from me but from our guiding coalition. This coalition was the school improvement team that included teachers from every grade level, special education and support staff, two parent representatives, a business partner, and a retiree from the community. Early in the school year, I took the instructional members of this team to a nearby, full-day workshop on professional learning communities that Rick presented for the Virginia Association for Supervision. By the end of the day, the team was ready to serve as advocates for the model to the rest our staff.

When we returned to school, the improvement team made a presentation to the faculty. I played no role in that presentation. Having teachers enthusiastically share the ideas of the PLC model with their colleagues was a powerful experience. The 15-minute presentation ended with a viewing of Rick's video, "How to Build a Professional Learning Community" (produced and distributed by Adlai Stevenson High School, Lincolnshire, IL). The faculty was spellbound. They applauded with enthusiasm and ultimately agreed to include professional learning community concepts in our school improvement plan.

Laying the Foundation

Our next important step was to build on the school's existing mission statement. We articulated a vision based on what the staff had said was important and where they wanted their school to go. We wrote collective commitments into our school improvement plans to define what each of us would do to move the school toward our shared vision. Finally, we identified two overarching goals for the school: improved student achievement in language arts and math as measured by state, local, and national assessments.

This complete foundation was written into our school improvement plan and endorsed by the faculty by the end of October, good evidence that establishing the mission, vision, values, and goals of a professional learning community does not need to be a lengthy, drawn out process. However, simply agreeing upon these statements does not create a professional learning community. We had to move beyond the words on this page to implement the structures that were necessary to build a learning community.

Aligning School Structures With the PLC Model

With the foundation in place, we began building the structures that would help us advance the PLC model. The first structure we created was to put the entire staff into teams. Most teachers were assigned to teams by grade level. Specialist teachers such as those in art, music, and physical education formed another team that would focus on the students they shared. Even non-instructional staff members were organized into teams.

Our next structural issue was creating a schedule that would allow us to address our priorities. When I built the master schedule (page 149), I considered how the schedule would provide three essential needs:

1. Consistent and large blocks of teaching and learning time: two consecutive hours every morning or afternoon of uninterrupted time for instruction. Teachers sought these large blocks of time so they could focus on essential knowledge the students needed to know.

2. Daily classes for all students in one or more "specials" which include music, art, physical education, guidance, library skills, and computer skills. The daily specials for

the students also gave their classroom teachers individual planning time to complete some of their routine tasks.

3. Weekly collaborative planning time for all teams: an hour to an hour and 10 minutes each week of uninterrupted collaborative team time.

When we developed the schedule, we realized we did not have enough specialists to free up collaborative team time for every team. Our creative solution was to develop a kindergarten and fifth-grade buddy system. The school nurse, librarian, and I would design and coordinate an hour lesson every week for our 140 fifth-grade and kindergarten students. Every fifth-grade student then became a peer tutor for his or her kindergarten buddy. Many of the lessons focused on character education, which is a part of the Virginia curriculum, and gave fifth graders a chance to serve as role models.

As part of each lesson, the kindergarten students would respond to a question or writing prompt designed to have them reflect upon the lesson. As the kindergarten students reacted to these prompts, their fifth-grade buddies wrote the responses in their journals. By the end of the year, these journals included photographs and entries, learning and memories from the peer tutoring. At our fifth-grade graduation ceremony, the kindergarten students sang three special songs for the fifth graders and the older students gave their little buddies the journals they had worked on together throughout the year. This was one way in which our school improvement efforts built strong relationships between our oldest and youngest students and created an hour each week for our fifth-grade and kindergarten teachers to meet and collaborate with each other.

Enhancing Team Productivity

Our school also needed to create structural supports to help teams be productive. We wanted to make sure that the things teams were doing would really affect student achievement. Each grade-level team was asked to do four things:

1. Analyze data on student achievement from the previous year.

2. Identify strengths and weaknesses of student performance.

3. Reach a consensus on the reality of past student achievement.

4. Identify a goal to enhance student achievement in both areas of our school-improvement plan: language arts and math.

Each improvement target had to be stated as a SMART goal, a goal that was strategic and specific, measurable, attainable, results-oriented, and time-bound. Every team had to answer the question, "What is a specific, measurable, results-oriented team goal that, if achieved, will contribute to the goals of our school?" Each team goal was then incorporated into our school improvement plan.

One example of this process involves the rubric our county developed for kindergarten students to assess their proficiency in the skills they would need for reading in first grade. During the 1999-2000 school year, 84% of our kindergarten students scored a 2 (the desired score) or higher on that rubric. The kindergarten team set a goal to move from the current reality of 84% of their students meeting the standard to 87% meeting the standard in the 2000-2001 school year. At the end of the year, 97% of the children in kindergarten had met the standard.

All of the teams experienced success in meeting their goals. On every single indicator that was set for that year, we either maintained our current score or surpassed it by as many as 16-18 points on local assessments and state test scores. Our focus on student achievement really did make a difference for our children.

One of the important aspects of a professional learning community is the alignment of these structures and activities, the school improvement plan, and the foundation of the school's mission, vision, values, and goals. These are not separate activities, but part of the same ongoing process. We agreed that we would focus on student achievement in two critical areas, and then we narrowed our efforts to the essential activities we felt would make a difference in student learning. Every team was asked to contribute to this schoolwide effort. Teachers understood how they could help the school achieve its goals if they stayed focused on their team goals.

Each team was free to identify the focus of their professional development activities, but those activities had to be linked directly to their team goals. I encouraged teachers to work together by providing them with funds and time to work on team projects. I also allowed participation on a team project to serve as an alternative to formal classroom observations by the principal. In other words, we tried to focus, coordinate, and leverage our efforts so teachers did not feel we were headed in multiple directions.

Another one of our strategies for providing structure for our teams was to help each team develop rules or protocols for how their members would work together. Although many of our teachers had worked together in the same building for years, they had never worked on a team or had to depend on each other to achieve a common goal. To help ease their transition into this teamwork, each team was asked to define the specific rules of operation they would follow to facilitate their work as a team. Each team could establish its own norms or protocols, but had to include the one protocol required of every team: self-evaluation as a team twice a year. The mid-year team reflection sheet that we used for this purpose is provided on page 144. We also evaluated their performance as a team at the end of the year so they could monitor their growth as a team and identify areas that could be improved.

Another tool that we added to the team process is the feedback sheet on page 143. Each team completed this sheet each week and gave it to me. I would read them, provide a handwritten response, and send a copy to each team member within 48 hours. This system maintained the lines of communication between the teams and me even when I did not attend their meetings. I also kept a notebook of the feedback sheets and asked each team to maintain a similar notebook. These notebooks provided great documentation of their topics and progress.

Each team was also asked to develop common skeleton lesson plans and pacing guides for each unit. Teachers agreed they would teach the same concepts and skills at the same time and use common assessments to monitor each student's mastery of those concepts and skills. These common lesson plans did not include specific strategies for teaching the skills. Each teacher could decide how he or she was going to teach the skills and concepts. Preserving this autonomy for the teachers was very important to us.

Parent involvement was also encouraged through the parent guides each team created for at-home student practice. Teams met with parents to distribute these guides and advise parents on how they could reinforce at home what students were being asked to learn at school.

One of the worst things that can happen to a team is to have members sit around a table and ask, "Why are we here?" I discovered that the best strategy to avoid this lack of focus is to ask each team to **produce** something. Our teams created SMART goals, lesson plans, pacing guides, rubrics, protocols, parent guides, common assessments, weekly feedback sheets, written summaries of student performance on assessments, and the strategies they would use to improve upon that performance.

Project PASS: Responding to Students Who are Not Learning

We never forgot that these activities were designed to improve student learning. Throughout the year, every time we met as a team or an entire faculty, we tried to ask ourselves, "What are we doing to ensure learning for all?" In Franklin County, as in every school district, all children are expected to learn. But if we truly believe that, we have to ask, "What are we going to do to make sure each child learns the essential material?" We decided that if we sincerely believed in learning for all, we had to address how we would respond when we had evidence a student was not learning.

We began with a description of the school's present response. In it we listed existing strategies and programs for assisting students who were having difficulty. We then held a brainstorming session on what more we might do. These discussions led to the creation of Project PASS (Preparing All Students for Success, see page 137), our school's systematic approach to providing all students and staff with the focus, time, and support to ensure learning for all.

At this point in our efforts to become a professional learning community, our teachers had clarified essential knowledge and skills for each grade level and unit of instruction. They had aligned their instruction with the specified learning objectives. They had designed and utilized team-made tests in the state assessment format. Training was provided to help teachers include higher order thinking skills in our local tests. We provided time for collaboration and job-embedded professional development. Teachers made the commitment to work together to improve student achievement.

Project PASS was designed to build on these initiatives. The following programs and strategies in Project PASS created a comprehensive approach to ensuring students received the help they needed:

- Promote learning through celebration.
- Use classroom incentives.
- Celebrate the learning of teachers.
- Involve parents.
- Provide additional time and support.
- Adopt the SOS—Save One Student—program.
- Consider additional interventions.
- Plan for short-term wins.

Promote Learning Through Celebration

Our school motto is "Hand in Hand We All Learn." As part of our decision to promote learning through celebration, we created a "Hand in Hand We All Learn" paper chain of little die cut paper dolls. Every time students at any grade level read a book, they wrote their name and the title of the book on a paper doll. We would add tape to the back of these dolls and link them to the ones already on a wall in the school. By the end of the year, those paper dolls stretched from the front door all the way through the three sections of our building. This "Hand in Hand We All Read" paper chain celebrated each student's achievement and also illustrated the reading that had been done by the school's students.

Use Classroom Incentives

We recognized daily curricular and extracurricular student achievement on announcements. If someone excelled at something in the classroom or won a chess tournament, softball game, or wrestling match, teachers or parents would write up announcements for us to celebrate in the morning as part of the general announcements. Quarterly awards assemblies recognized all children for their accomplishments. High-performing students were acknowledged, but we also gave BUG (Bringing Up Grades) awards to honor and encourage students who showed improvement. Good citizenship and work habits were also awarded to ensure we recognized as many students as possible. Parents and community members were invited to join in this celebration of learning.

Celebrate the Learning of Teachers

Thirty minutes of every faculty meeting were devoted to allowing teachers who had attended a workshop, visited another school, or read a great article to share their learning. Teams were asked to share successes and insights. We tried to eliminate the "adminis-trivia" from faculty meetings and focus more on staff development.

Involve Parents

Parents were great partners with us, and we tried to foster open, two-way communication with them. Each classroom sent home a weekly student work folder with feedback from the teacher so parents knew what their children were learning and how they were performing. Each grade-level team created a parent newsletter that highlighted upcoming events and recognized students who had achieved certain standards in the classroom. We provided parents with teacher-made materials that gave the parents tools and tips to reinforce at home the essential knowledge and skills students were expected to learn at that grade level. We held parent workshops at each grade level and organized the parent back-to-school night so students could show off their school, classrooms, and work to their parents.

Provide Additional Time and Support

One of the most important things we did to demonstrate our commitment to learning was to provide additional time and support for students who struggled to master the skills of any unit. We identified these students through an ongoing item analysis of the common assessments developed by each team. This analysis enabled us to assess each student's mastery of the key skills that had been identified at their grade level. An analysis worksheet is provided on page 148.

Once we identified the students who were having difficulty, we provided them with additional time and support through a tutorial program. Part-time floating tutors were hired with state remediation funds. Many of these tutors were mothers who had been substitute teachers in our building and had shown a commitment to our school. To facilitate tutoring, each grade-level team identified a block of time every day when students could be pulled out of class by a tutor to receive additional support. Tutors could also be assigned to take over a class during that block of time to allow the classroom teacher to work directly with students who needed extra attention. Tutorial periods were always scheduled when the rest of the class was assigned to silent sustained reading, guided practice, or listening to the teacher reading aloud. Students receiving tutorial services did not miss direct instruction of essential knowledge and skills.

Adopt the SOS Program

The SOS program—Save One Student—was adopted to help the children in our school who were not getting adequate parent support. We confidentially identified those students and then assigned one staff member per child to monitor, encourage, and support his or her student. Staff members made a commitment to meet with their child at least three times per week, even if it was only to touch base with the student by asking, "How did you do on your homework last night? Let's see what you did." The staff member might also read to the student or have lunch with him or her.

Consider Additional Interventions

When all else failed, we would convene our child study team to consider additional interventions we could initiate at the school level or seek the parent's permission for a case study to explore the need for special education. Interventions might include additional diagnostic testing, preferential seating, oral administration of tests, extending time for test taking, and so on.

Plan for Short-Term Wins

Our school improvement team recognized the importance of demonstrating and celebrating initial success early in our improvement process. As John Kotter, management consultant and Harvard professor, wrote in *Leading Change* (1996): "Without short-term wins too many people will give up or join the resistance. Creating short-term wins is different from hoping for short-term wins" (p. 11).

To create short-term wins, we built into our school improvement effort several measurable indicators that we felt fairly certain we could achieve before the end of the year. Then we celebrated our progress. For example, when the central office endorsed and commended our school improvement plan, we celebrated. When our tracking of student data at the end of each 9 weeks indicated our students made progress, we celebrated.

In short, the specific strategies and support systems of Project PASS were designed to provide a timely response to every student who was experiencing difficulty in learning.

Communicating Priorities Through Attention

Throughout all of these efforts and initiatives, I was very mindful of my responsibility to help us stay focused on student learning. I tried to avoid sending mixed messages. I tried not to be overwhelmed by the day-to-day managerial demands of the principalship so I could consistently communicate my personal commitment to student learning. As Warren Bennis and Burt Nanus wrote in *Leaders: The Strategies for Taking Charge* (1985): "Leaders convey what really counts in an organization by how they spend their time, the questions they ask, their reactions to critical incidents, and what they reward."

I knew that the key to the effectiveness of my communication was what I did rather than what I said. I discovered that the communications audit in *Professional Learning Communities at Work* (1998) was a useful tool to help me reflect on what I was doing to clarify the priorities for Boone's Mill. The questions in that audit include the following:

What do we plan for?

Remember, every teacher and every team had a hand in our school improvement plan, a specific plan designed to increase student achievement in our school. The plan required every team to identify and pursue SMART goals. And we developed a plan to provide additional time and support for any student who had initial difficulty in learning.

What do we monitor?

We monitored every child's achievement of the essential knowledge and skills outlined by the teachers. We also monitored every team's weekly work and progress toward its goals.

What do we model?

We modeled the commitment of our official school pledge which asked us to respect each other (page 140). We modeled a focus on learning and a willingness to also be learners. We modeled an attitude of "whatever it takes," which became the unofficial motto of our school. We were committed to doing whatever was necessary to help all of our children become successful.

What questions do we ask?

The 15 critical questions that Rick presents (page 146) became the guiding questions for our teams. As a school we were driven by the following questions:

- What knowledge and skills should each student acquire from each unit of instruction?

- How do we know if each student has mastered the intended outcomes?

- How will we respond when a student has initial difficulty in achieving the standards we have established?

How do we allocate resources?

We made a conscious effort to allocate and align our time, money, and energy in a way that would give us the biggest return on our investment of our scarce resources.

What do we celebrate?

We celebrated learning at every turn. We looked for opportunities to celebrate the achievement of our students and our teachers.

What are we willing to confront?

I had to learn to confront behaviors that interfered with what we needed to do. I would confront behaviors individually in my office and would never embarrass a staff member, but I also had to make it clear to an individual or a team when change was mandatory. Team members would also confront their own behaviors if they were not living up to the norms that they had established for themselves at the beginning of the year. If we began to disregard norms at our faculty meeting, I could simply ask, "Are we adhering to our norms?" and we would get back on track.

Setting Our Sights Higher

Finally, we wanted to establish some stretch goals—goals we knew we would not accomplish in that first year, but would motivate us to strive for sustained improvement. Some of our stretch goals included applying for an Excellence in Education award, a regional award in Virginia. Another goal is to investigate and go through the Blue Ribbon School Award process. Our school song and PTO motto call for one last stretch goal: Boones Mill will become the best school in the United States of America. This goal is no longer just the words of a song. Together, our stretch goals represent a collective pledge to continue working together, hand in hand, until every student in our school is achieving at high levels.

I encourage each of you to continue working hand in hand toward school improvement. I believe professional learning communities are our best hope and our most promising model for sustained school improvement. I hope that what I have shared will encourage and inspire you to build a professional learning community in your school.

Chapter 4

A Conversation With the Authors

National Educational Service (NES): The idea of schools functioning as professional learning communities has generated a lot of excitement. One of the most frequently asked questions is this: Where do I start? What would you recommend for school leaders who are just getting started in the process of transforming their schools into professional learning communities?

Becky: We started the process by engaging small groups of teachers in dialogues about their perceptions of the school's past and present. I tried to get a really good picture of both the historical context and the current reality of the school from the perspective of the teachers. Then I asked the teachers to describe the school they wanted to become by asking, "What can we do to become an even better school?" So the shared vision we were developing from these conversations was based on our assessment of our current reality. I also shared articles summarizing best practices for school improvement to provide a common framework and vocabulary for our dialogues.

So, as we began to act on our school's new vision, we held on to the things that were working well and wove the learning community elements into tasks with which teachers were already familiar. We tried to keep our focus on learning, which I think is the key. We did that through the collaborative efforts of the teachers, so that when they came together they had tasks that required them to think about how the work of their team was going to impact the learning of the students in their class-rooms.

Bob: I think another idea, for people who are just interest-ed in getting started, is to find out everything you can about schools that are functioning as professional learning commu-nities. Visit some of those schools. Read about professional learning communities. Watch the videos. I think you really need a deep knowledge base before you really start the process.

Rick: It is so important to honor the current context and wrap some of the PLC concepts into the existing practices of the school. Too often teachers see PLC as another new thing and as a revolutionary change in direction, as opposed to an evolutionary process. They are much more amenable to an approach that says, in effect, "Here is a way to enhance the good things that we've been doing."

But Bob's point is so well taken in that we cannot just con-tinue to do what we have done. We must alter and extend our practices, and the changes should be based upon building shared knowledge regarding best practice. The leaders of the process do not have to have all the answers, but it's critically important that they ask the right questions. As Becky men-tioned, when she began asking her teams to work together, she helped articulate and focus the questions she wanted them to be able to answer. By asking those questions she helped them to begin working like the collaborate teams of a professional learning community.

Finally, while it's important to honor the current context and to build shared knowledge, it is also very, very important that we move as quickly as possible to get people to start taking action, to help them experience doing things differently. Not until they begin to act in accordance with the tenets of a professional learning community will they begin to understand them at a deeper level.

NES: In your work you frequently mention how important it is for those who are directing the process of developing professional learning communities to develop a "conceptual understanding" or "conceptual framework" from which to work. What do you mean by this?

Bob: It's really a continuation of the earlier point I made about a knowledge base. I think it's awfully important for our leaders in professional learning communities to understand that this isn't a "program" that we're adopting for our school. It's really a way of thinking. If you think about the way professional learning communities work you have to ask the question, "How is this going to affect everything we do?" And it will affect many of the things you do. It will affect budgeting. Ask, "How are these requests for funds going to move us towards our vision of the school we want to become?" It's going to affect staff development. It's going to affect your teacher evaluation program, your administrator evaluation program. So the leader has to be able to connect all these dots and see the relationship between the different aspects of schooling in the district and the characteristics of a professional learning community.

Becky: We continue to build the knowledge base—the conceptual framework at Boones Mill—in several different ways. From the start of the process teachers were provided with articles that explained the characteristics of a professional learning community. Those articles gave us common vocabulary and concepts that provided the framework for our faculty discussions. A core group of teachers from our school improvement committee attended a workshop that Rick conducted on building a professional learning community. They came back and shared the knowledge with their colleagues and helped to guide them throughout the process. We continue to refer to sections of Rick and Bob's book when the information is pertinent to existing situations or issues that the teachers are confronting. Building this conceptual framework must be ongoing, not a one-shot deal.

NES: Would you elaborate a little bit on the relationship between the district leadership and the individual building leaders as this process gets underway? Just how important is district leadership and what are some of the things that need to be addressed at the district level in order to support individual schools in becoming professional learning communities?

Rick: It is important that district leaders support the efforts of schools that are attempting to become professional learning communities, but I don't think it is absolutely critical. I have seen schools develop as professional learning communities despite general indifference from district leadership, but it required yeoman effort, heroic effort, on the part of those schools.

District leaders should accept responsibility for creating conditions that foster learning communities in schools. At the same time, they should recognize that school improvement happens one school at a time. District leadership can play a huge role in creating learning communities in their schools if district leaders come to a deep understanding of loose/tight leadership. The district has to be willing to be "loose" on many of the individual aspects of creating a professional learning community in terms of how the process gets played out. The process need not and should not use a cookie-cutter approach. Different schools can approach the challenge in different ways. Individual schools will need a high degree of autonomy in order to pull this off. But at the same time, the district leadership must be "tight" on certain areas. District leaders have every right to advise building leaders that there are certain elements of their job they consider critical, certain expectations that must be met.

I would include at least four things that I think district leaders need to be "tight" about with the building leaders if they're trying to promote learning communities. First, they should insist that the learning of each student will be monitored on a timely basis in every school. The strategies of the monitoring could vary from building to building in terms of how it gets done, but the fact that it will get done should not be subject to discussion. Second, district leaders should insist that each school develop its own systematic way of responding to students who are not learning by providing them with additional time and more support during the school day. Third, district leaders should insist that teachers work together in collaborative teams that are pursuing very specific results that the teams have had a voice in articulating. If we're going to build a results-oriented school in a results-oriented district, we have to have results-oriented teacher teams who are focusing on setting some very specific goals for student achievement. Finally, district leaders should ensure that each teacher is being provided useful information on how his or her students did in meeting an agreed-upon standard on a valid test in comparison to all the other students in the school who are attempting to achieve that same standard. If district leaders would just get "tight" on those four things and then free building leaders from the constant pursuit of new district initiatives, they could really foster learning communities in their schools.

Bob: A way to think about the themes that run through Rick's comments is that it certainly helps individual schools if, at the district level, the leaders of the district have modeled the expectations that they have for schools. For example, it's very helpful if at the district they themselves have a vision of the district; they have a set of district values and so forth. Also, setting up priorities is important. It's very, very difficult for an individual school to become a professional learning community if the district leader shows a different set of priorities, or priorities that are in another direction, that may hinder individual schools in becoming professional learning communities. But most important, I think what Rick is commenting on is this culture of high expectations that can flow from the district level. That's very, very helpful in encouraging individual schools to become professional learning communities or behave in ways that professional learning communities behave.

NES: What about those principals and teachers who are in districts that lack strong leadership at the district level? Is there any hope for them? Can they still transform their schools into professional learning communities?

Rick: I say absolutely, yes! And I think my answer probably runs contrary to conventional thinking. But too often people who read about, learn about, or attend workshops on professional learning communities, walk out saying, "Well, I hope someone in the district gets this done." The principals think,

"Well, I hope the superintendent does this." Or a department chairman walks out saying, "Well, I hope the principal does it." There is a tendency to want to assign responsibility to someone else. But professional learning communities can be created in individual schools in which the district is really indifferent to the concept. Milbrey MacLaughlin's research on high schools makes it clear that even in a high school that's indifferent to the concept of professional learning communities, individual departments within the school can be functioning as a professional learning community at a very high level. It is certainly much more difficult without external support, but it is doable. I advise not to wait for somebody else in the organization to create a learning community, but rather, look at your own place in the organization and start working at it there.

Bob: We've actually had the opportunity in a few cases to observe where individual schools have taken the initiative to become professional learning communities, and have in fact influenced the leadership at the district level. So not only can individual schools do this, but they can also have an impact on the entire district by getting out front, showing results, and spreading the news.

Becky: The effort to transform every school into a professional learning community was not a division-wide focus initially in our site-based system. The success of Boones Mill teachers and students generated a great deal of interest in the PLC model, and now all schools in our division are being asked to take steps to incorporate PLC concepts. The change does not have to come from the top down. In fact, an individual school can spur changes that trickle up.

NES: While we are on this subject of leadership, just how important is the "leadership factor"?

Bob: We believe the leadership factor is everything. In the worst cases, we've worked in schools and school districts where people want to adopt the professional learning communities' framework to compensate for and support weak leadership. This seldom works. The ideals and characteristics of a professional learning community are simply not strong enough. In fact, I know of no program that's strong enough to compensate for weak or ineffective leadership. So leadership is the dynamic that pulls together all the various elements of a professional learning community and maintains and supports them. How well things get done in a professional learning community will depend on the quality of leadership. The leadership is the lubrication that's going to make this work or not work.

NES: Do leaders in professional learning communities behave differently than their counterparts in more traditional schools? If so, in what ways?

Bob: I think in more traditional schools we tend to think of all the tasks that have to get done, all those management things that certainly have to be done. But in a professional learning community, while recognizing that tasks have to be done, we focus on different priorities. We make sure that there is a collaborative effort to have our vision in place, the kind of school we're seeking to become. We've collaboratively developed value statements on how we're going to behave in our school. Then the role of the leader in a professional learning community becomes promoting, protecting, defending those values, confronting behavior that is incongruent with those values, and celebrating the behaviors that are best examples of those values.

So, in that way, the leadership behavior in a professional learning community is quite different.

NES: Another question that is frequently asked is this: "We've started the process of reculturing our schools to become professional learning communities, but I have a few teachers with a 'bad' attitude about any change that is proposed. What can I do to change their attitudes?" How do you respond to this type of question?

Rick: We have to dig a little deeper and ask what has shaped this person's "bad" attitude. All of us have attitudes—good, bad, or indifferent—and those attitudes are shaped by our history and by our experiences. We have experienced certain things that, over time, have shaped the way we look at the world. The question then becomes, What led us to have the experiences that shaped our attitudes? Typically, our experiences flow from our actions. We have acted in certain ways, or behaved in certain ways. Those actions led to an experience. If, over time, we replicate that experience enough, it will form an attitude.

Leaders who say, "I need to change this person's attitude," are trying to break into the cycle at the wrong point. Psychologists say it's seven times more difficult to change an attitude than a behavior. So, the short answer to the question, "How can I change someone's attitude?" is simple: focus on his or her behavior rather than attitude.

When we are able to help people behave in ways that will lead to new experiences, over time we can help shape their attitudes. If we provide people with a new experience that's contrary to their expectations, contrary to their assumptions, and contrary to their past experiences, then we have created a moment of cognitive dissonance where they might be willing to rethink some of those attitudes and assumptions. If leaders will simply focus on action and behavior, as opposed to attitude, they will move in the right direction. That is why we urge schools to identify value statements as "core commitments" to behave in certain ways rather than writing values as belief statements. We want people to be very explicit about how they are prepared to behave in order to move their school in the direction of a learning community.

Bob: Focusing on behavior, rather than focusing on attitude, allows the school to move forward. There are some people in leadership positions who feel they can't move forward with becoming a professional learning community until everybody's attitude is in favor of the steps that need to be taken, so then they wait and wait and wait, and nothing gets done. Focusing on behavior allows you to move forward, and the attitudes will come along later.

NES: One last question to tie back into the issue of leaders having a conceptual framework: What are the roles of various support areas such as transportation, food service, clerical, maintenance, etc. in districts and schools that are attempting to become professional learning communities? Do they have roles to play?

Bob: Not only do they have a role to play, but it's a critical role. Every department, every area that's associated with the school needs to understand what a professional learning community is and how people behave in professional learning communities. For example, we've worked in school districts where the transportation department, or the food service department, has developed vision statements. They make a commitment to how they're going to behave to support the school in becoming a professional learning community. But most importantly, these various departments are seeking out best practices, they're trying those practices out in their department, and they're setting goals on steps they want to take to improve. Every aspect of a school district can become a professional learning community. We use the term professional learning community in its broadest sense. It's not just student learning. It's learning throughout the district.

Becky: Each person in our division and in our school has at least one job-alike peer. The members of our custodial staff, clerical staff, or food services department are expected to function as a team in much the same way as our instructional staff. They are asked to incorporate continuous learning processes into their routines so they become more proficient in fulfilling their responsibilities. Furthermore, they have agreed to support student learning in every way possible. For example, each full-time member of the staff has "adopted" one student and monitors that student's performance at school. The members of the support staff play a critical role in our school-wide effort to further our shared vision.

NES: Associated with the importance of strong leadership is the need for professional learning communities to develop strong, meaningful, collaborative cultures. What are some first steps one might take in an attempt to embed collaboration into the school culture?

Becky: We understand that you cannot invite people to collaborate and expect everyone to volunteer his or her time. So each person is assigned to a grade-level or department team. Every team is provided time for collaboration during the school day so that the collaboration is viewed as a part of their job rather than an add-on. Teams are asked to complete certain tasks that focus their attention on the critical questions of the learning process: What do we want kids to learn? How will we know when they've learned it? and How do we respond when they don't?

One of the first tasks our teams addressed was developing team norms to help each member monitor his or her personal contribution to the team process and goals. Our teams continue to evaluate themselves twice a year to assess their adherence to their norms and progress toward their team goals.

One of the strategies we use to help teams maintain their focus on student learning is asking each team to develop and present certain products, which should be a natural outgrowth of their work as a team. These products include common assessments, parent tools and tips for at-home student practice, curriculum guides, pacing guides, and analysis of student performance on assignments and assessments. One of the most significant products each team generates is a student achievement goal and an action plan for achieving that goal. This emphasis on asking teams to "produce" helps teams maintain a sense of shared purpose and priorities. Our teams never have to ask the question, "What are we supposed to do?"

Rick: We must do more than simply organize people into what we say are "teams" and then order them to collaborate. All the wonderful things happening in Becky's school, and the wonderful focus of her teams, are directly attributable to the fact that she helped them identify very specific parameters, very specific priorities, and very specific tasks to accomplish. We can build collaborative cultures, but we can't do it simply by asking people to collaborate, or even creating the structure that requires them to meet periodically. We have to take steps to make sure those meetings become productive and the teams begin to see benefits from working together.

NES: Leadership and collaboration are essential for establishing trust. Do you have any suggestions regarding establishing trust in a professional learning community?

Becky: Trust is built over time. It goes back to the idea of leaders modeling their priorities through their behaviors. Teachers learn to trust their leaders when leaders do the things they are asking others to do. Leaders must also continually build those trusting relationships within the collaborative groups. People, over time, will see that the norms leaders set and the commitments they make really do drive the work. They must recognize that leaders are going to do what they say they'll do, rather than just talk about it.

Bob: I feel the same way about issues related to trust as I do about issues related to attitude. You need to get started and let your behavior be congruent with the values you profess, and then you build trust. I simply don't think it makes sense to wait until everyone trusts each other, and then take off on our mission to become a professional learning community. Trust is something that's built incrementally over time. Of course, this puts a tremendous responsibility on the part of leaders to continually manage their own behavior so that they can build trust and lead others. I think that the first time that the leader's behavior is incongruent with what they've been professing, it tends to just wipe out any trust that's been built. So you have to be very, very careful to make sure that your behavior is congruent with those values and commitments you've made.

Rick: A leader has to make sure that his or her behavior is congruent with the things that he or she says are important. As a matter of fact, we've tried to create a brief instrument to help leaders assess whether or not their actions are aligned with what they are saying. The instrument is based on the premise that people within an organization come to recognize the priorities of a leader by what that leader does rather than what he or she says.

Some of the questions upon which we ask leaders to reflect are: What am I planning for in the school? Am I sharing plans that will help us move in the direction of the school we're trying to become? What are we monitoring in our school? Am I focusing on the right things? If I contend that student learning is the priority in our school, are we in fact monitoring each student's learning on a timely basis? If building a collaborative culture is critical, am I monitoring the work of our teams? What do I model? Are my actions consistent with what I have said are my priorities? What are the questions I am presenting for people to consider? Are those questions directing the attention of the school to the most important issues? How am I allocating the resources that are available to me, particularly the resource of time? Am I providing the time for people to focus on the things that we say are most important? What are we celebrating in our school through stories, ceremonies, and rituals? Is celebration a part of our culture? And last, what am I willing to confront? Do I care enough about our priorities that I am willing to confront those who disregard them?

When leaders reflect upon these questions and assess whether or not they are acting in ways that are consistent with what they have said are the priorities, over time people will extend the trust leaders need to be effective in this process of improving a school or school district.

NES: You pointed out that collaboration in a professional learning community is different from collaboration in a more traditional school in a number of ways. One important way that you've touched upon is through the use of "collective inquiry." Just what is collective inquiry?

Bob: In a professional learning community we use collaborative teams to engage in collective inquiry and action research. Perhaps the best way to think of collective inquiry is to think of it in these terms: we expect collaborative teams to seek out best practice. We have a tendency in more traditional schools, I think, to have teachers collaborate and essentially average their opinions about what they think about a particular problem or issue or direction that we need to take. But in a professional learning community we do the opposite. We expect collaborative teams and teachers to seek out best practice. They read articles. They get on the Internet. They join professional societies. They attend conferences and workshops. Most importantly, they visit other sites that have a reputation of doing things really well, so they benchmark against other schools or other departments. So there's this constant search for best practice. By doing this, a professional learning community creates a culture of continuous improvement.

Rick: The issue is not just being engaged in collective inquiry. Throwing teachers together and asking them to "collaborate" is a recipe for disaster. It is important that a staff is engaged in collective inquiry, but whether or not the inquiry benefits the school will depend on the nature and topics of the dialogue. There are schools where teachers engage in collective inquiry on such topics as, "What is wrong with these kids?" or "What textbooks should we be using?" or "Should students be allowed to wear hats?" Discussions of this nature will not bring about gains in student achievement. As Bob said, in a professional learning community, collective inquiry will focus on a constant exploration of best practice in our profession. It centers on those critical questions Becky mentioned earlier: What is it we want the students to learn? How will we know when they have learned it? And how will we get better results based on the evidence that we have in front of us? So, in short, the focus of the collaboration is at least as important as the fact that we collaborate.

NES: Educators in professional learning communities are expected to engage in "action research." Could you share some examples of action research?

Rick: One of the examples that had a profound impact on us at Stevenson was an ongoing debate about the merits of placing students in remedial programs versus placing them in the mainstream program and providing them with more support. This was a raging debate on our faculty with people perfectly willing to weigh in with their opinions. Ultimately, the English department agreed to put the respective theories to the test in an action research project. Some students who ordinarily would have been placed in the remedial program were randomly assigned to mainstream-level English classes and provided additional time and support to be successful. Other similar students were assigned to our traditional remedial English courses. We tracked both student achievement and student attitudes throughout the year. At the end of that year it was absolutely, overwhelmingly crystal-clear that putting kids into the regular program and giving them time and support was a superior strategy. Not only did students perform better on every academic indicator we monitored, but they also felt very good about what they had accomplished. That little action research project conducted in the English department really spurred us to abandon a schoolwide approach of sorting and selecting students. It had a profound impact.

Becky: At Boones Mill every team has an action research project that is tied directly to their team's student achievement goal. For example, teachers throughout our building are focusing on helping their students achieve better results in language arts. So they engage in a yearlong action research project with their teammates to examine and implement best practices in language arts instruction. As they learn new strategies, they "test" these new practices in their classrooms. Teachers support each other as they implement the strategies and work together to evaluate the impact on student learning.

To encourage teachers to participate in this kind of ongoing experimentation, action research has been incorporated into the division's model of teacher evaluation. So, a teacher engaged in action research is completing the requirements of the supervision and evaluation model and gaining state re-certification points in the process. Our teachers benefit personally from action research; however, the biggest benefit is their increased ability to make a difference in student learning.

NES: It's often suggested that one way to build trust is through "consensus decision-making." While you recognize the importance of collaboration and consensus, you often have words of caution regarding "reaching consensus." What are your concerns and what suggestions do you have as to how one might avoid some of the pitfalls associated with consensus decision-making?

Rick: Our primary concern is that people confuse the term "consensus" with "unanimity." In many instances school leaders are saying that they have not arrived at consensus until every single person on the faculty or every single person in the group is in agreement. There is a difference between consensus and unanimity. We think it is important for schools to arrive at an organizational definition of what they mean by "consensus" to avoid an ongoing debate about whether or not the group has arrived at a conclusion. Some people may walk out of a meeting convinced the group had reached consensus while others may walk out equally convinced that no agreement was reached. I learned the hard way here at Stevenson when I went through a process that led to what I defined as consensus, and our teachers' union informed me that they disagreed. So it's important that the people in a school have clarity on what they mean by the term.

A definition of consensus that has helped our school improvement effort simply states: we have arrived at consensus when, first, all points of view have been heard, and second, the will of the group is evident, even to those who most oppose it. This definition has some serious implications. There are different strategies we can use to ensure that all points of view have been heard. Typically, someone merely poses the question and then everyone in the group starts weighing in with their opinions. While this strategy helps people sharpen their debate skills, it is not particularly effective in moving a group toward consensus. We have found it is more effective to pose the question, and then ask half of the group to brainstorm all the possible benefits of the proposal and the other half to identify all the possible objections. Participants are asked to reserve their personal responses and focus on the task of generating all the pros and cons. This strategy gets all the arguments and ideas out on the table without rancorous debate and without people staking out early positions in front of the group. Not until all the possible points of view have been presented are people asked to give an indication of where they stand. When the person who is the most opposed to an idea looks around the room as people indicate their level of support and acknowledges that the rest of the group is in favor of going forward, we have arrived at consensus. We think this standard of consensus, particularly in a large group, is far superior to the premise that the school cannot take action until everyone endorses the idea. Schools that wait for everyone to get on board the school improvement train are unlikely to ever leave the station.

Bob: One of the central themes that runs throughout this book is the idea, "How do I get started?" I think implied in that question is that there are things that sometimes prevent us from getting started. Sometimes we wait until everybody's attitude is how we want it to be, or we wait until we build a level of trust so that everyone trusts each other and the processes we're engaging in. Another thing that keeps us from moving forward is having an unrealistic view of consensus—we simply can't move forward until everyone agrees on the directions we're going to take. In that kind of thinking, one or two faculty members can hold an entire school hostage. By adopting a working definition of consensus that allows us to engage in deep, meaningful discussion, and at the same time recognize the will of the group, it certainly helps us to move forward in becoming a professional learning community.

NES: Of course, one of the first areas in which collaboration is essential is in the development of the mission statement. Would you talk just a little about the practical aspects of developing a mission statement?

Becky: Most districts and/or schools have already developed a mission statement to articulate their purpose. The pledge of most mission statements is "learning for all students." The departure for learning communities is found not in the language of the mission statement, but rather in the fact that they not only promise learning for all, but they also live that promise. They focus on those three critical questions we keep repeating: What is it we want all students to learn? How will we know they have learned it? And how will we respond when they do not learn initially? The mission statement in a learning community is not found in the words on a piece of paper, but rather in the daily actions of the members of the school.

Bob: One of the practical aspects I've experienced in working with schools that have drawn up mission statements is that there's a tendency to spend far too much time on it. I have had the experience of working in schools that will say, "This year we're going to focus on developing our mission statement." It simply does not take that long to actually write a mission statement that provides a school with a focus on learning. What does take time are the corollary questions that are associated with that—the ones that Becky just mentioned. Those corollary questions are really going to make a mission statement meaningful anyway.

Rick: Those familiar with our work know that we talk about laying the foundation of a professional learning community. The foundation includes a clear sense of purpose or mission, a shared sense of vision of what we're trying to become as a school, an agreed-upon set of collective commitments or values that state the actions we will take in moving our school in the desired direction, and specific goals that serve as benchmarks to monitor our progress.

Becky built that entire foundation in her school, all four pieces—mission, vision, values and goals— and had consensus throughout her faculty within 4 months of taking her position as principal. Her school represents a classic example of moving through the philosophical and conceptual to the point at which people are ready to take action. She could have taken a full year on the mission statement, and then another year on a vision statement, and so on, but it would have been the fifth year before they were doing anything differently. Instead, they were changing practices and learning from their experience in less than 6 months.

Bob: I think that in education, generally, we have a tradition of getting bogged down in the philosophical issues. And it's just so difficult for us to realize that these aren't that difficult, that we can talk about these, and we can reach some consensus and we can move on. So we would suggest that the leadership set a timetable that's reasonable, certainly, but at the same time allow the school to move forward.

NES: Following the mission statement, you've stated that schools should develop a shared vision. Many vision statements are full of education jargon and are essentially useless. How do you make a vision document meaningful?

Bob: I think the most critical way you make a vision statement meaningful is simply by using it. So often, we spend an enormous amount of time writing these vision statements, and then they tend to be ignored, filed away. But in a professional learning community we do the opposite—we use the vision statement as the driving catalyst in a number of areas. An example is our administrator evaluation program. If we are going to evaluate administrators in a school district, shouldn't we evaluate them in terms of how well they're moving their school towards the vision of what they've collaboratively decided they want to become? The same is true with budgeting. Budgeting is one of the key ways we set priorities. So shouldn't there be an alignment between budgeting and the allocation of resources and the vision we set for our school? And certainly staff development. Shouldn't our vision statement be one of the things, if not the key thing, we look at as we develop our staff development activities? How will the staff development activities that we've planned for our school and school district move us toward the vision we seek to become? So the key to making a shared vision statement useful and meaningful is to actually use it.

NES: On the topic of corollary questions—there has been a slight change in your thinking about these corollary questions that makes a mission statement meaningful. In the past you have referred to two questions, now you focus on three key questions. What is your thinking about this third corollary question?

Rick: Initially we focused on the two questions: What is it we want students to learn? And how do we know if they are learning it? What we have come to understand over time is the importance of the question, so what happens when we find out that students aren't learning? What steps are we taking to get better results, how are we responding to those students to give them additional time and support, and what are we doing as a team to improve the levels of student learning? Assessing how a school responds to students who are not learning may be the single best indicator of its development as a learning community. Despite the best efforts of teachers, every year in every school—including professional learning communities—there will be those students who simply do not "get it" initially. Educators acknowledge this reality. It never catches them by surprise. So the relevant question becomes, what happens then? Will we provide a systematic response to give those kids more time and support? Will we give teachers the information that helps them identify where students are not learning well and the time and support to help them improve on results? Or will we continue to leave this critical question of response to each teacher to resolve individually, knowing it will result in huge discrepancies in the way we treat students and the levels of their learning?

Bob: In more traditional schools we address the issue of how we are going to respond by encouraging teachers to help students and assist students who aren't learning. But in a professional learning community, while recognizing that what individual teachers do is certainly important, we also recognize that there's only so much an individual teacher *can* do. It's the collective efforts of the teachers together, those who collaboratively develop schoolwide plans to assist and support students in their learning, that makes a professional learning community real in terms of addressing this third corollary question.

NES: I know you feel that it is very important for teachers to collaboratively develop common assessments. Why do you think this is so important? Becky, how did you do this in your school?

Becky: After the teachers at Boones Mill had initially identified essential knowledge and skills by content areas, they worked together to decide how to assess whether the children had learned what teachers wanted them to know. So the teams made formative assessments using the format of the state test whenever possible. Teachers were able to diagnose each student's level of understanding and to identify any student who needed additional time and support to acquire the essential learning. This intervention could then take place prior to the state assessment. Furthermore, students were becoming familiar with the format of our high-stakes state test.

Teachers at Boones Mill have a very clear understanding of what each student must know and be able to do as a result of each unit of instruction. They have the benefit of common assessments to help them identify students who need additional assistance. But while outcomes and assessments are common, instructional strategies are left to the discretion of each individual teacher. All teachers have the autonomy to use their own creative strategies and teaching styles, provided they help students demonstrate mastery of essential learning on common assessments.

Rick: We are really getting to the heart of the matter of why common assessments are so critical. If you accept the premise that one of the key questions that professional learning communities focus upon is "How do we know if students are learning?" then locally developed common assessments provide the answer to that question in a timely way. Results from state assessments are typically unavailable until the end of the school year—too late either to provide the interventions for students who have not learned or the feedback to teachers whose students are struggling.

So it's critically important from the standpoint of fulfilling our purpose of learning for all students to use timely, common assessments so we can identify those students who need the additional time and support. Both formative and summative assessments give us information, but formative assessments are to summative assessments what a physical examination is to an autopsy. A summative assessment at the end of the year can give us good information about the program—here's what our students did well or didn't do well. We can use that information when we teach the content to the next group of students, but that does nothing for those kids who have left us and have not mastered the intended skills. Common, teacher-made, teacher-driven formative assessments are critical in providing timely feedback on the learning of every individual student.

A second benefit of common assessments is the way they facilitate the team process. Again, we define a team as a group of people working interdependently to achieve a common goal. When teachers clarify essential outcomes, develop common assessments, and set standards they want all students to achieve by test and by subtest, they are in a position to establish goals that can only be achieved if each member contributes. They can begin to function as an effective team, and effective teams are essential to the collaborative culture of a learning community.

The last reason we think common assessments are so critical is because they provide each teacher with feedback on how his or her students did in achieving an agreed-upon standard on a valid test in comparison to similar students attempting to achieve the same standard. Each teacher becomes more aware of what his or her students learned well and where they struggled, and each can learn whether or not these patterns were evident with all students. Armed with this powerful information, a teacher can become more insightful regarding changes he or she might make to improve instruction. If you think of all the critical elements—the focus on learning, a collaborative culture where people work together in teams, a focus on results—they are all enhanced by these common assessments, which serve as a real catalyst for a school committed to becoming a professional learning community. I would go so far as to say that if you do not have common assessments, you dramatically reduce the chances your school has for ever becoming a professional learning community.

NES: Practitioners often feel that developing a set of shared values or commitments is the most difficult document to complete. At the same time, you have frequently observed that it is perhaps the most important aspect of reculturing schools. Do you have any suggestions for those who are at this stage of developing a professional learning community?

Rick: We would offer four suggestions to schools that are at the point where they are trying to articulate collective commitments. First, the commitments should be linked directly back to the vision statement. This is not an independent, abstract discussion. It is, rather, a very focused and purposeful discussion that says, since we have agreed that this is the school we want to become, what are the very specific behaviors we must demonstrate in order to become this school? The commitments flow directly from a shared sense of what we have already agreed we are trying to become as a school.

The second suggestion is to limit the number of collective commitments to a handful; five or six is plenty. If a school develops too many, people will forget them and they will fail to impact day-to-day operations. As we say in our workshops, even God limited us to ten guiding principles with the Ten Commandments.

A third critical assumption is that these commitments should be stated as actions and behaviors rather than beliefs. Over and over again, this book emphasizes that it is the actions and the behaviors of people that create professional learning communities. It is not just what they talk about. It is not what they say they believe. It is how they act. Some school improvement models specifically recommend writing values as beliefs. We disagree. Value statements should describe what you are prepared to do; for example, "We commit to do the following things in order to help us become the school that we want to become."

Lastly, avoid the tendency to tell other groups what their commitment should be. Typically, teachers want to say, "Well, if the administration would just commit to do these things, we could become a better school." Administrators say, "Well, if the teachers would just commit to do these things . . . " We always want to tell the other guy what their commitments should be. But we can't make commitments for the other guy. We can only make them for ourselves. So the challenge facing those who are considering developing commitments is to embrace personal responsibility rather than focusing on deficiencies in others.

NES: In regards to reculturing schools, you have written that "confrontation" and "celebration" are two ways important values are imbedded into a school culture. How does this work on a day-to-day basis?

Becky: Our celebrations focus upon our collective commitments to learning for both students and staff. Each day begins with the recitation of the Boones Mill pledge, which reminds us that "Hand in Hand We All Learn." We then celebrate both academic and non-academic student achievements during daily school announcements, in both grade-level and school-wide newsletters, and at quarterly award assemblies. Examples of awards include the principal's honor roll for those who achieve straight A's, the A/B honor roll, the BUG (Bringing Up Grades) awards, "most improved" in each content area, citizenship, work habits, and perfect attendance. In other words, every student at Boones Mill has the opportunity to be recognized and celebrated.

We also celebrate adult learning. Faculty meetings include "share the learning" time when teams can share new ideas, products, and insights that have resulted from their collaboration. With the help of our parent teacher organization, we also celebrate our collective efforts through special breakfasts and luncheons for the entire staff. We make a conscious effort to build a sense of the Boones Mill "family."

Our collective commitments also serve as a guide for confrontation. We have agreed to behave in certain ways that will lead us to achieve our shared vision, and we have an obligation to address those who do not behave in ways that honor those agreements. Sometimes team members confront inappropriate behavior as they reflect on paying attention to the norms.

Sometimes the school improvement committee challenges the results we are achieving when those results are inconsistent with our school goals. Then, of course, the principal must confront behaviors of individual teachers when they are not demonstrating the commitments that leaders have made to students and the school.

NES: Many of the questions practitioners have focus on the technical aspects of becoming a professional learning community. Yet, you frequently talk of the importance of "passion." Why do you think this is so important and how does this get played out in a professional learning community?

Rick: Passion is critical in this process for two reasons. First of all, the process is inherently messy. It never runs flawlessly and we never get it right the first time. Schools only persist through some of the sticky points when things are not going as planned if the people within them are passionate about the process. School leaders are notorious for staying with an initiative only until it gets difficult. When the going gets tough, they conclude that the initiative does not offer the magic bullet they were seeking, and they head off in search of a new, simple solution. The difficult times are inevitable and can be overcome only through the tenacity and persistence that are byproducts of passion.

The second reason why passion is so critical is that most of us are not going to be driven or motivated by the notion of raising student test scores 3% on the state tests. Data-driven goals represent indicators of the progress we are making, but it is not the numbers that evoke passion. Most educators enter their profession because they hope to make a difference in the lives of kids. So the best leaders appeal to the heart. They tell an ongoing story with specific examples of how the collective efforts of the staff are helping students overcome obstacles and achieve their dreams. They remind staff that the most important things the school hopes to accomplish can be achieved only if they work together. When people feel successful, when they feel that they are making a difference, when they feel a sense of connectedness, they will put forth the effort essential to sustaining the improvement process through tough times. So leaders must appeal to passion if they expect people to persist.

Bob: The idea of passion ties right back to some comments that were made earlier in this conversation about the importance of leadership. If you think about it, leaders do a lot of things, but one of the most important things they do is motivate and inspire. Unless we can do that to get people excited and passionate about the endeavor, then our leadership efforts are probably not going to be effective.

NES: One final question: Teachers have been bombarded with many fads through the years. How do we keep the idea of professional learning communities from becoming just another fad? Can you share your thoughts about the importance of persistence?

Bob: We think that in many schools, teachers—when provided with the ideas of a professional learning community, or really any initiatives—have the attitude of "this too shall pass." When you think about it, that really shouldn't be surprising to us because in most cases that simply has been their experience; these new ideas and initiatives only last, as Rick mentioned, until the going gets tough, and then we look for something else. But in a professional learning community we do the opposite. If we have taken the time to have deep and meaningful collaborative discussions about the kind of school and school district we seek to become, then we believe it is our obligation to persist over time to achieve that vision, and so we don't jump ship at the first little fad that comes along. In fact, we ask the opposite question. Regarding fads and so forth, while we obviously want to experiment and try new things, we filter these new initiatives through a framework of, "Will these new initiatives help us achieve the vision of the kind of school or school district we are seeking to become?" So our vision of our school or our school district becomes the standard in which we judge new initiatives, new ideas, new activities, and so forth. That way it helps us to not just jump on the bandwagon of every new fad that comes along.

Rick: If people approach the learning community concept as a canned program—"Here are the six things you have to do in order to become a learning community"—it will become just another fad. What the PLC model offers is a process, not a program. Furthermore, the process it presents is ongoing and never ending. We worked at this for 10 years at Stevenson High School, and did all the things that we talked about in the book, without ever referring to a "professional learning community." Becky launched this initiative in her school and had it up and running with a solid foundation and people working in teams for several months before anyone in the school ever used the term "professional learning community." She did not walk in and say, "I've been to a workshop and found the recipe that will transform our school." She simply initiated a process that helped people begin to experience the practices of a PLC. Those looking for a quick and easy solution for improving a school must look elsewhere. This model offers a process for addressing the very difficult and challenging task of implementing and sustaining initiatives that help all kids achieve at higher levels and help all teachers become the very best teachers they can be.

Chapter 5

A Call for Action

At the conclusion of our workshops we often ask participants to complete an evaluation to give us feedback on the program, to indicate their degree of enthusiasm for the PLC concepts, and to identify the "next steps" they are prepared to take to advance those concepts in their school or district. Very discernible patterns have emerged over the years. Respondents are typically very positive about the call for schools with shared mission, vision, values, and goals where teachers work together in collaborative teams engaged in collective inquiry and action research, and where continuous improvement processes help the school focus and improve upon results. They heartily endorse the PLC model, and they would love to see it implemented in their schools; however, they are not always optimistic.

The reason for this lack of optimism typically depends upon the respondent's position in the school district. Teachers report that they would love to see their school function as a PLC, but that a lack of administrative support would prevent it from happening. Principals report they would love to see their schools functions as a PLC, but teacher opposition and interference from the central office will prevent it from happening. Central office staff report they would love to see their schools function as PLCs, but ineffective principals and resistant teachers will prevent it from happening.

Isn't it ironic how frequently we question the willingness of others to do what must be done to improve our schools, and in doing so, absolve ourselves of the responsibility for taking action? Perhaps it is time we head the words of Helen Keller who said, "I am only one, but still I am one; I cannot do everything, but still I can do something; I will not refuse to do something I can do."

If we have one hope in writing this book, it is that it will spur those who read it to "do something"—regardless of their position within their organizations. Principals have created effective learning communities in their schools despite central office indifference to their efforts. Department chairpersons have created powerful learning communities in schools with structures and cultures that are not conducive to the model. Teachers of a particular grade level have banded together to create dynamic collaborative teams that have attracted the interest of their colleagues. What these innovators had in common was not position, but the willingness to accept personal responsibility for doing what they could do.

Wishful thinking and good intentions do not improve schools. Even serious reflection and meaningful dialogue impact school improvement only to the extent that those within the school are persuaded to act differently. Thus, our goal in presenting the ideas, examples, strategies, and stories offered in these chapters was to inspire readers to action.

We recognize that we have not presented a specific, step-by-step process for making the transition to a professional learning community. As we noted in the Introduction, the path to becoming a PLC is non-linear and there is no "one right way" to proceed. We do believe, however, that the basic themes woven throughout the book provide practitioners with the conceptual framework to guide their journey.

So, begin the process of school reculturing by making "learning" rather than "teaching" the fundamental purpose of your school. Focus on the three key questions: What do we expect students to learn? How will we know what they have learned? And how will we respond when students don't learn?

Then build the strong foundation of a professional learning community. Activities and initiatives will gain meaning if they are pursued in the context of collaboratively developed mission, vision, values, and goals. If a staff has a clear sense of the fundamental purpose they are working to achieve—when they can describe the school they are trying to create to better fulfill that purpose, when they make collective commitments to move their school in the intended direction, and when they establish specific targets and benchmarks to monitor their progress—they have the benefit of steady beacons to guide them on the sea of change.

Build a deep, meaningful collaborative culture in your school. Organize your school around collaborative teams that work interdependently to achieve common goals. And, remember that virtually all schools set goals, but in professional learning communities collaborative teams set goals that focus on the right things—the key questions related to learning.

Use the team structure to foster a collaborative culture in your school. Be certain that the members of each team are working interdependently to achieve common goals, and provide each team with the parameters, resources, and information essential to their effectiveness.

Constantly communicate priorities. Promote, protect, and defend the vision and values of your school through attention. Assess your effectiveness in communicating priorities by asking the following questions on an ongoing basis: What do we plan for? What behaviors and attitudes do we model? What do we monitor? What do we celebrate? What are we willing to confront? How do we allocate our time, energy, and money? What are the questions that are driving our school?

Finally, we would encourage those who seek to reculture schools into professional learning communities to be hard-nosed about some rather "soft" ideas. Resolve to create a culture where people care for each other, where people are tender with one another's feelings, where people make extraordinary efforts to support and help each other. Create a culture that is characterized by positive attitudes. Things will go wrong. Plans will fall apart. Problems are inevitable. There will be ample opportunities to quit, to pursue some new fad that offers the quick and easy solution. The question we must be prepared to answer is not, "How can we ensure that we never experience problems?" but rather "How will we respond when the problems arise?" Even the most formidable obstacles to becoming a professional learning community can only slow you down. You are the only one that can stop yourself permanently.

So, go forth with passion, persistence, enthusiasm—and more than a little grace. Know that the undertaking is important and significant and can transform the lives of countless children and adults. We wish you the best as you begin the journey.

Chapter 6

Artifacts

The following pages contain examples, handouts, and assessment tools that can be used as schools make the cultural shifts to becoming professional learning communities.

Critical Questions for Team Consideration 146
These questions help teams focus on topics that are correlated with gains in student achievement.

Student Achievement Goal-Setting Worksheet 148
This sheet is designed to help teams identify SMART goals and the plans they will implement to achieve these goals.

Master Schedule for Instruction 149
Boones Mill's Master Schedule shows how the school found the time for collaboration.

Franklin County Public Schools Comprehensive School Improvement Plan 150
The Boones Mill Elementary School improvement plan illustrates how schoolwide goals are translated into specific team goals.

Quality Indicators Questionnaire for Successful School Improvement Planning 156
While virtually all schools do some sort of improvement planning, the quality of the planning process can be improved by asking some basic questions about how plans were developed. This brief questionnaire is an example of the kinds of questions that can be used to improve the quality of the planning process.

The Professional Learning Community Continuum

Robert Eaker, Richard DuFour, Rebecca DuFour

When school personnel attempt to assess their ability to function as a learning community, they are likely to create a simple dichotomy—the school either functions as a professional learning community or it does not. The complex process of school improvement cannot, however, be reduced to such a simple "either/or" statement. It is more helpful to view the development of a PLC along a continuum: Pre-initiation, Initiation, Developing, and Sustaining. Each element of a PLC, as shown in the following pages, can be assessed during the four stages of the continuum:

Pre-initiation The school has not yet begun to address a particular principle of a PLC.

Initiation An effort has been made to address the principle, but the effort has not yet begun to impact a "critical mass."

Developing A critical mass has endorsed the principle. Members are beginning to modify their thinking and practice as they attempt to implement the principle. Structural changes are being made to align with the principle.

Sustaining   The principle is deeply embedded in the school's culture. It represents a driving force in the daily work of the school. It is so internalized that it can survive changes in key personnel.

Assess the position of your school on each area of the continuum. Identify examples and illustrations to support your placement.

Shared Values:
How Must We Behave to Advance Our Vision?

Pre-initiation   Staff members have not yet articulated the attitudes, behaviors, or commitments they are prepared to demonstrate in order to advance the mission of learning for all and the vision of what the school might become. If they discuss school improvement, they focus on what *other* groups must do.

Initiation   Staff members have articulated statements of beliefs or philosophy for their school; however, these value statements have not yet impacted their day-to-day work or the operation of the school.

Developing   Staff members have made a conscious effort to articulate and promote the attitudes, behaviors, and commitments that will advance their vision of the school. Examples of the core values at work are shared in stories and celebrations. People are confronted when they behave in ways that are inconsistent with the core values.

Sustaining   The values of the school are embedded in the school culture. These shared values are evident to new staff and to those outside of the school. They influence policies, procedures, and daily practices of the school as well as day-to-day decisions of individual staff members.

Goals: What Are Our Priorities?

Pre-initiation   No effort has been made to engage the staff in setting and defining school improvement goals related to student learning. If goals exist, they have been developed by the administration.

Initiation   Staff members have participated in a process to establish goals, but the goals are typically stated as projects to be accomplished, or are written so broadly that they are impossible to measure. The goals do not yet influence instructional decisions in a meaningful way.

Developing   Staff members have worked together to establish long- and short-term improvement goals for their school. The goals are clearly communicated. Assessment tools and strategies have been developed and implemented to measure progress toward the goals.

Sustaining   All staff pursue measurable performance goals as part of their routine responsibilities. Goals are clearly linked to the school's shared vision. Goal attainment is celebrated and staff members demonstrate willingness to identify and pursue challenging stretch goals.

Collaborative Culture: Administrator/Teacher Relations

Pre-initiation   Questions of power are a continuing source of controversy and friction. Relationships between teachers and administrators are often adversarial.

Initiation   Efforts have been made to reduce friction by clarifying "management rights" and "teacher rights." Both parties are protective of intrusion onto their turf.

Developing   Administrators solicit and value teacher input as improvement initiatives are developed and considered, but administrators are regarded as having primary responsibility for school improvement.

Sustaining   Staff are fully involved in the decision-making processes of the school. Administrators pose questions, delegate authority, create collaborative decision-making processes, and provide staff with the information, training, and parameters they need to make good decisions. School improvement is viewed as a collective responsibility.

Collaborative Culture: Teachers Working Together

Pre-initiation   Teachers work in isolation. There is little awareness of what or how colleagues are teaching.

Initiation   Teachers recognize a common curriculum that they are responsible for teaching, but there is little exchange of ideas regarding instructional materials, teaching strategies, or methods of assessment.

Developing   Teachers function in work groups that meet periodically to complete certain tasks such as reviewing intended outcomes and coordinating calendars.

Sustaining   Teachers function as a team. They work collaboratively to identify collective goals, develop strategies to achieve those goals, gather relevant data, and learn from one another. Unlike a work group, they are characterized by common goals and their inter-dependent efforts to achieve those goals.

Parent Partnerships

Pre-initiation　There is little or no effort made to cultivate a partnership with parents. Parents are either ignored or viewed as adversaries.

Initiation　An effort is made to keep parents informed of events and situations at school in order to secure parental support for the school's efforts.

Developing　Structures and processes for two-way communication with parents are developed. The parental perspective is solicited on both schoolwide issues and matters related directly to their own children.

Sustaining　The school-parent partnership moves beyond open communication. The school provides parents with information and materials that enable parents to assist their children in learning. Parents are welcomed in the school and there is an active volunteer program. Parents are full partners in the educational decisions that affect their children. Community resources are used to strengthen the school and student learning.

Action Research

Action research is investigation carried out by teachers and practitioners in real-work settings to answer a question or assess the impact of a practice or method on improving student learning.

Pre-initiation　While individual teachers may try experiments in their own classrooms, no structures to support, assess, or share their findings are in place. Many staff members have no knowledge of or involvement in action research.

Initiation Some staff members participate in pilot action projects. The sharing of findings is largely informal.

Developing Staff members have been trained in action research methods and conduct action research to improve their professional practice. Findings generated by this research are beginning to influence classroom practices.

Sustaining Topics for action research arise from the shared vision and goals of the school. Staff members regard action research as an important component of their professional responsibilities. There are frequent discussions regarding the implications of findings as teachers attempt to learn from the research of their colleagues.

Continuous Improvement

Pre-initiation Little attention is devoted to creating systems that enable either the school or individual teachers to track improvement. The school would have a difficult time answering the question, "Are we becoming more effective in achieving our shared vision?"

Initiation A few people in the school are tracking general indicators of achievement, such as mean scores on state and national tests. Positive trends are celebrated. Negative trends are dismissed or suppressed.

Developing   Individual teachers and teaching teams gather information that enables them to identify and monitor individual and team goals.

Sustaining   Everyone in the school participates in an ongoing cycle of systematic gathering and analysis of data to identify discrepancies between actual and desired results, goal setting to reduce the discrepancies, developing strategies to achieve the goals, and tracking improvement indicators.

Focus on Results

Pre-initiation   The results the school seeks for each student have not been identified.

Initiation   Results have been identified, but are stated in such broad and esoteric terms that they are impossible to measure. Improvement initiatives focus on inputs—projects or tasks to be completed—rather than on student achievements.

Developing   Desired results have been identified in terms of student outcomes and student achievement indicators have been identified. Data are being collected and monitored within the school or district. Results of the analysis are shared with teachers.

Sustaining   Teams of teachers are hungry for information on results. They gather relevant data and use these data to identify improvement goals and to monitor progress toward the goals.

Summary Checklist:
Tracking and Assessing Cultural Shifts

Robert Eaker, Richard DuFour, Rebecca DuFour

1. Collaboration

Teacher isolation   Teacher collaboration

0   1   2   3   4   5   6   7   8   9   10

Suggestions for Improvement:

2. Developing a Mission Statement

Generic   Clarifies what students will learn

0   1   2   3   4   5   6   7   8   9   10

Suggestions for Improvement:

3. Developing a Vision Statement

Belief statements such as,   Statements that clarify how the school will
"We believe all kids can learn"   respond when students do not learn

0   1   2   3   4   5   6   7   8   9   10

Suggestions for Improvement:

Statement is ignored   Statement is used as a
                                                        blueprint for improvement

0	1	2	3	4	5	6	7	8	9	10

Suggestions for Improvement:

4. Developing Value Statements

Linked to random values   Linked to vision

0	1	2	3	4	5	6	7	8	9	10

Suggestions for Improvement:

Articulated as beliefs   Articulated as behaviors
                                                   and commitments

0	1	2	3	4	5	6	7	8	9	10

Suggestions for Improvement:

Focus on others   Focus on self

0	1	2	3	4	5	6	7	8	9	10

Suggestions for Improvement:

5. Developing Goal Statements

Random   Linked to vision

0	1	2	3	4	5	6	7	8	9	10

Suggestions for Improvement:

| | | | | | | | | | | Translated into measurable |
| Impossible to assess or measure | | | | | | | | | | performance standards |

| 0 | 1 | 2 | 3 | 4 | 5 | 6 | 7 | 8 | 9 | 10 |

Suggestions for Improvement:

| Not monitored | | | | | | | | | | Monitored continuously |

| 0 | 1 | 2 | 3 | 4 | 5 | 6 | 7 | 8 | 9 | 10 |

Suggestions for Improvement:

| | | | | | | | | | | Designed to produce short-term |
| Goals are not reachable | | | | | | | | | | wins and stretch aspirations |

| 0 | 1 | 2 | 3 | 4 | 5 | 6 | 7 | 8 | 9 | 10 |

Suggestions for Improvement:

6. Emphasis on Learning

| Primary focus on teaching | | | | | | | | | | Primary focus on learning |

| 0 | 1 | 2 | 3 | 4 | 5 | 6 | 7 | 8 | 9 | 10 |

Suggestions for Improvement:

										Collaboratively agreed upon
Each teacher independently										curriculum focuses on what
decides what to teach										students are expected to learn

| 0 | 1 | 2 | 3 | 4 | 5 | 6 | 7 | 8 | 9 | 10 |

Suggestions for Improvement:

Curriculum overload								Reduced content; meaningful content taught in greater depth		
0	1	2	3	4	5	6	7	8	9	10

Suggestions for Improvement:

All assessments individually developed									Collaboratively developed assessment	
0	1	2	3	4	5	6	7	8	9	10

Suggestions for Improvement:

7. Collective Inquiry

Decisions about improvement strategies made by "averaging opinions"								Decisions are research-based with collaborative teams of teachers seeking out "best practices"		
0	1	2	3	4	5	6	7	8	9	10

Suggestions for Improvement:

8. Action Research/Experimentation

Effectiveness of improvement strategies is externally validated. Teachers rely on those outside the school regarding what works.							Approaches are internally validated. Teams of teachers try various approaches and collaborate about how the approaches impact student learning.			
0	1	2	3	4	5	6	7	8	9	10

Suggestions for Improvement:

Emphasis is given to how teachers
liked various approaches.

Effects on student learning are
the primary basis for assessing
various improvement strategies.

| 0 | 1 | 2 | 3 | 4 | 5 | 6 | 7 | 8 | 9 | 10 |

Suggestions for Improvement:

9. Teachers as Leaders

Administrators are viewed as
being in leadership positions,
while teachers are viewed as
"implementors" or followers.

Administrators are viewed as
leaders of leaders. Teachers are
viewed as transformational leaders.

| 0 | 1 | 2 | 3 | 4 | 5 | 6 | 7 | 8 | 9 | 10 |

Suggestions for Improvement:

10. School Improvement Planning

School improvement plans focus
on a wide variety of things.

School improvement plans focus
on a few important goals that
will impact student learning.

| 0 | 1 | 2 | 3 | 4 | 5 | 6 | 7 | 8 | 9 | 10 |

Suggestions for Improvement:

Often, the goal is to "get the plan
turned in." Then the plan is ignored.

The school improvement plan
is the vehicle for organized,
sustained school improvement.

| 0 | 1 | 2 | 3 | 4 | 5 | 6 | 7 | 8 | 9 | 10 |

Suggestions for Improvement:

11. Celebration

Celebration is infrequent and when recognizing teachers, almost always focuses on groups.

Celebration is frequent and singles out individuals as well as groups.

0	1	2	3	4	5	6	7	8	9	10

Suggestions for Improvement:

Celebration and recognition occur when students reach an arbitrary standard.

In addition to celebration and recognition when a standard is met, celebrations recognize "improvement."

0	1	2	3	4	5	6	7	8	9	10

Suggestions for Improvement:

Recognition is limited to few.

The school works hard to "create" winners and celebrate their success.

0	1	2	3	4	5	6	7	8	9	10

Suggestions for Improvement:

Celebration and recognition are random.

Celebrations are linked to the vision and values of the school and improved student achievement.

0	1	2	3	4	5	6	7	8	9	10

Suggestions for Improvement:

12. Persistence

Improvement efforts frequently shift as new fads or trends come along.

The school is committed to "staying the course" in attainment of the school's vision. New initiatives are only implemented if it is determined that the change will help the school achieve its vision of the future.

0	1	2	3	4	5	6	7	8	9	10

Suggestions for Improvement:

The leader focuses on managing various day-to-day events and activities.

The leader's role is to promote, protect, and defend the school's vision and values and to confront behavior that is incongruent with the school's vision and values. The leader recognizes and celebrates behavior that best exemplifies the school's values.

0	1	2	3	4	5	6	7	8	9	10

Suggestions for Improvement:

10 Steps in Becoming
A Professional Learning Community:
A General Guide

Robert Eaker, Richard DuFour, Rebecca DuFour

1. **Acknowledge Collaboration:** The first, and perhaps most important step is really a concept. Everyone involved in the PLC must understand that each issue and problem that comes up along the road to becoming a PLC will be addressed by teams of teachers working collaboratively together.

2. **Know PLC Concepts:** Everyone must have a clear understanding of the concepts and characteristics of schools that function as professional learning communities.

3. **Develop Shared Mission, Vision, Values, and Goals:** The staff of each school should develop shared mission, vision, values (commitments), and goals taking into account input from all appropriate groups. This must be done well, in writing, understood by all, and (most importantly) used.

4. **Communicate a Mission of Student Learning:** The mission statement may take many forms, but it must communicate that the central mission of the school is student learning.

Often it is helpful to reduce the mission statement to a shorter, more motivational slogan.

After the mission statement is adopted, the school should develop plans to have teams of teachers address the following questions for the school:

- What do we want students to learn in each subject, grade level, or course?

- How will we assess what students know and can do?

- What is our plan for responding to students who aren't learning?

5. **Describe a Vision of Excellence:** The vision statement should describe the school you seek to become. The vision statement is really a description of what the staff believes excellence looks like for each of the various aspects of schooling, such as school climate, leadership, curriculum, technology, student involvement, parental involvement, etc.

6. **Use the Vision Statement:** The vision statement must be used. All key issues, such as budgeting, curriculum, initiatives, organizational structure, etc., should be linked to the school's vision. In other words, how will these changes help the staff move toward its vision?

7. **Link Value to Vision:** The value or commitment statements should be linked directly to the vision statement. As each area of the vision statement is analyzed, ask the question, "If we are to become this kind of school, what attitudes and behaviors must we exhibit as a staff?"

- This is most important: the leader's role is to communicate, promote, protect and defend the commitment statements, and address behavior that is incongruent with the statements.

8. **Focus on Short-term and Long-term Goals:** The collaborative development of goals addresses the question of what steps must be taken and when. Hence, the school must focus on both short-term and long-term goals. The school improvement plan is the vehicle for developing, implementing, monitoring, and assessing the goals. Plans should be developed to recognize and celebrate incremental improvement as goals are achieved.

9. **Engage in Research-based and Data-driven Plans:** The school improvement plans should be research-based and data-driven. Hence, teams of teachers are engaged in seeking out best practices, trying out these practices, and collaboratively analyzing the effects of the practices on student learning.

10. **Expect a Cyclical Process:** This process must be cyclical, internalized, and always focus on improving student learning. In other words, the process should be part of how the school operates everyday. More than anything, the process of becoming a professional learning community ultimately means reculturing schools.

Mission Statements

The New Catholic High School Mission

The New Catholic High School is a Catholic, secondary level, diocesan educational institution that continues the mission of the Church to form and inform people in Christian values and tradition as taught by the Catholic Church.

It is the mission of the New Catholic High School to:

- Motivate students to lead exemplary lives that reflect Catholic values.

- Expand students' knowledge and scholarship by creating a learning environment that promotes academic excellence and an appreciation of the beauty of God's creation.

- Create a diverse learning community dedicated to the mutual support of students, parents, faculty, and staff and a commitment of service to others.

Franklin Special School District Mission

Excellence in teaching and learning for all.

Foundation Statements

Boones Mill Elementary School Mission

It is the mission of Boones Mill Elementary School to provide its students with opportunities designed to meet individual needs and to ensure that every child has experiences that promote growth in each area of development. Through mutual respect within the total school community, our children will grow and learn in a positive atmosphere where faculty, staff, parents, and students together are enthusiastic about the teaching/learning process.

Vision

We believe that the most promising strategy for achieving the mission of BMES is to develop our capacity to function as a professional learning community. We envision a school in which staff:

- Unite to achieve a common purpose and clear goals;

- Work together in collaborative teams;

- Seek and implement promising strategies for improving student achievement on a continuing basis;

- Monitor each student's progress; and

- Demonstrate a personal commitment to the academic success and general well-being of all students.

Collective Commitments

In order to achieve the vision of a school that functions as a professional learning community, the Boones Mill staff has made the following collective commitments:

- Align and utilize state resource guides, SOL Blueprints, and Division Curriculum Guides for instruction;

- Develop, implement and evaluate team Professional Enhancement Plans to target specific instructional areas identified by student data analysis;

- Engage in meaningful, job-embedded staff development to enhance professional skills;

- Initiate individual and small group instructional programs to provide additional learning time for students;

- Provide parents with resources, strategies, and information to help children succeed academically;

- Utilize a variety of instructional strategies to promote success for all students; and

- Develop and implement local assessments using state and national standardized testing formats.

Goals

- Improve student performance in language arts in each grade level as measured by performance on local, state, and national assessments.

- Improve student performance in math in each grade level as measured by performance on local, state, and national assessments.

Project PASS:
Preparing All Students for Success

PURPOSEFULLY ALIGN CURRICULUM, INSTRUCTION, ASSESSMENT, **&** STAFF DEVELOPMENT

- Utilize State Resource Guides, The Virginia Standards of Learning (SOL) Blueprints, and Division Curriculum Guides to clarify essential knowledge and skills by grade level.

- Align daily instruction with specified learning objectives.

- Design and utilize teacher-made tests in the SOL Assessment format.

- Reinforce content & skills in "Specials" classes (i.e., Art, Music, Physical Education, Guidance, Library, Computers) and Pull-out Programs (i.e., Speech, Special Education Resource), and Cultural Arts Presentations.

- Provide staff with job-embedded opportunities for ongoing collaboration and professional development directly related to student achievement goals.

- Create a master schedule that provides protected instructional blocks, time for teacher collaboration, and individual teacher planning.

A CTIVELY PROMOTE A CLIMATE OF ACHIEVEMENT: INCENTIVES AND CELEBRATIONS

- Display a "Hand in Hand We All Learn" paper "people-chain" throughout the school, recognizing each student who meets specific academic goals.

- Recognize student curricular and non-curricular achievements on daily school announcements.

- Publish names of students who meet achievement goals in classroom and school newsletters.

- Provide individual student recognition in such areas as most improved, citizenship, and academic achievement in quarterly awards assemblies.

- Provide individual incentives and quarterly recognition assemblies for students who meet individual and classroom reading goals.

- Share professional learning and achievements at weekly team meetings and monthly staff meetings.

S TRUCTURE STRONG PARENT PARTNERSHIPS

- Create systems for consistent, two-way communication between home and school (i.e., notes, phone calls, visits).

- Send student work folders home each week for parent review and signatures.

- Provide parents at each grade level with homework tips, study guides, and specific resource materials.

- Conduct grade-level parent workshops to clarify intended outcomes and provide strategies that enable parents to reinforce the intended learning at home.

Support Students Who Need Additional Time to Learn

- Conduct item analysis of student achievement data to identify individual and group strengths and weaknesses.

- Provide time and structure for students who need additional support to learn the intended skills/content.

- Create peer-tutoring systems within classrooms and grade levels.

- Implement a student buddy system to give younger students assistance from older students.

- Utilize staff to provide daily tutorial services for individual students and small groups.

- Utilize computer-based, individualized math and reading programs available in each classroom and computer lab.

- Organize parent volunteers, business partners, senior citizens, and high school and college interns to serve as mentors and tutors.

- Implement SOS Program—Save One Student—to provide personal encouragement and support to certain students.

- Convene the Child Study Team to plan additional interventions.

Boones Mill School Pledge

We the Boones Mill School Community pledge to respect ourselves, to respect others, and to respect our school.

We know that respect means:

R   Responsibility

E   Effort

S   Spirit

P   Pride

E   Enthusiasm

C   Courtesy

T   Teamwork

We will work hard together because
"Hand in Hand We All Learn"

All Kids Can Learn!

All kids can learn based on their ability.

We believe that all students can learn, but the extent of their learning is determined by their innate ability or aptitude. This aptitude is relatively fixed, and as teachers we have little influence over the extent of student learning. It is our job to create multiple programs or tracks that address the different abilities of students, and then guide students to the appropriate program. This ensures that students have access to the proper curriculum and an optimum opportunity to master material appropriate to their ability.

All kids can learn if they take advantage of the opportunity to learn.

We believe that all students can learn if they elect to put forth the necessary effort. It is our job to provide all students with this opportunity to learn, and we fulfill our responsibility when we attempt to present lessons that are both clear and engaging. In the final analysis, however, while it is our job to teach, it is the student's job to learn. We should invite students to learn, but honor their decision if they elect not to do so.

All kids can learn if we accept responsibility for ensuring their growth.

We believe that all students can learn and that it is our responsibility to help each student demonstrate some growth as a result of their experience with us. The extent of the growth will be determined by a combination of the student's innate ability and effort. It is our job to encourage all students to learn as much as possible, but the extent of their learning is dependent on factors over which we have little control.

All kids can learn if we establish high standards of learning that we expect all students to achieve.

We believe that all students can and must learn at relatively high levels of achievement. It is our job to create an environment in our classrooms that results in this high level of performance. We are confident that with our support and help, students can master challenging academic material, and we expect them to do so. We are prepared to work collaboratively with colleagues, students, and parents to achieve this shared educational purpose.

Team Feedback Sheet

Name of Team:_____

Meeting Date: _____

Team Goal(s): _____
_____
_____
_____

Team Members Present: **Team Members Absent:**
_____   (List reason for each absence)
_____   _____
_____   _____
_____   _____
_____   _____

Topics/Meeting Outcomes:

Questions/Concerns:

Administrator: _____
Date: _____

Mid-Year Reflections Survey

Boones Mill Elementary School

Grade-Level/Team: _____

Date: _____

Please reflect on your experiences as a member of an instructional team this school year and respond to the following questions:

	Strongly Agree	Agree	Neutral	Disagree	Strongly Disagree

1. I know the norms and protocols established by my team.

Strongly Agree	Agree	Neutral	Disagree	Strongly Disagree
5	4	3	2	1

Comments: _____

_____

_____

2. Members of my team are living up to the established norms and protocols.

Strongly Agree	Agree	Neutral	Disagree	Strongly Disagree
5	4	3	2	1

Comments: _____

_____

_____

	Strongly Agree	Agree	Neutral	Disagree	Strongly Disagree

3. Our team maintains focus on the established team goal(s).

	5	4	3	2	1

Comments: _____

_____

_____

4. Our team is making progress toward the achievement of our Professional Enhancement Plan.

	5	4	3	2	1

Comments: _____

_____

_____

5. The principal promotes a collaborative culture in our school.

	5	4	3	2	1

Comments: _____

_____

_____

Critical Questions for Team Consideration

Team Name: _____

Team Leader: _____

Date: _____

Consider the following statements in relationship to your team and indicate the level to which the statement is descriptive of your team:

This is not true of our team.	This is true of some but not all of the team.	Uncertain.	Our team has addressed this issue.	We have consensus and act in accordance with our consensus.
1 2	3 4	5 6	7 8	9 10

1. _____ Each member of our team is clear on the intended outcomes of our course in general as well as on the specific outcomes of each unit.

2. _____ We have aligned the outcomes of our course to statewide goals and to high-stakes tests.

3. _____ We have identified the prerequisite knowledge and skills needed to master the intended outcomes of the course or unit.

4. _____ We have identified strategies and created instruments to assess whether students have the prerequisite knowledge and skills.

5. _____ We have agreed on how to best sequence the content of the course to help students achieve the intended outcomes.

6. _____ We have agreed on the criteria we will use in judging the quality of student work in key areas of our course such as writing, speaking, and projects.

7. _____ We have taught students the criteria we will use in judging the quality of their work and have provided them with examples.

8. _____ We have developed formative assessments that help us identify strengths and weaknesses of individual students.

9. _____ We have developed summative assessments that help us assess the strengths and weaknesses of our program.

10. _____ We have established the proficiency level we want all students to achieve on our summative assessments.

11. _____ We have identified content and/or topics that can be eliminated so we can devote more time to essential curriculum.

12. _____ We have analyzed student achievement data and established measurable team goals that we are working together to achieve.

13. _____ We have identified team norms or protocols to guide us in working together.

14. _____ We adhere to our team norms.

15. _____ We are continually looking for new ways to help students achieve at higher levels.

Student Achievement Goal-Setting Worksheet

Team Name: _____   **Team Leader:** _____

Question being addressed by the stated goal: _____

Identify a Student Achievement SMART Goal for your team (Specific, Measurable, Attainable, Results Oriented, and Time-bound): _____

Action Steps	Designation	Time Frame	Evaluation
What steps or activities will be initiated to achieve this goal? What products will be created?	Who will be responsible for initiating or sustaining the action steps?	What is a realistic timeframe for each phase of the activity?	What evidence will you present to show that you are making progress toward your goal?

Master Schedule for Instruction

The Master Schedule provides large blocks of protected instructional time for all classes; daily "specials" classes for all students (i.e., art, music, physical education, guidance, library, or computers); individual planning time for all instructional staff; and weekly collaborative planning for all instructional staff.

Boones Mill Master Schedule for Instruction 2001–2002

Time	Monday					Tuesday				Wednesday					Thursday				Friday				
	L	C	M	G	PE	L	C	G	PE	L	C	G	A	PE	L	C	M	PE	L	C	G	A	PE
8:15–8:40	Breakfast, Early Morning Work, Accelerated Reader Tests, Bookstore, & First Virginia Banking Project																						
8:40–8:50	Tardy bell followed by Moment of Silence, Pledges, and Morning Announcements																						
8:50–9:25			2-S	2-W		2-W	2-H		2-S	2-W	2-S	2-S	2-H		2-S	2-S	2-W		2-S		2-W	2-W	2-H
9:30–10:05		3-F	2-H				3-J	3-D	3-F	3-D	3-F	3-J	3-J	3-D	3-F	3-F	3-J	3-D	3-F		2-H	2-S	2-W
10:10–10:45		3-J	3-D				3-D	3-J	3-J	3-J	3-D		3-F	K-DI	K-R	K-DU	3-F	K-DI	1-H	3-D	3-D	3-F	
10:50–11:25	1-J	1-R	1-H			1-R	1-H		1-J	1-J	1-J	1-R	1-H	1-H	K-DI		1-R	1-H	K-DI	K-R	K-DU	1-J	K-P
11:30–12:05	K-DU	K-R	K-P			K-P	K-DI	K-DU	K-R	K-DU	K-P	K-DI	K-R	1-R	K-R		1-J	1-R	K-R	K-DI	K-P	1-R	K-DU
12:10–12:45	Lunch schedule begins at 10:45 and ends at 1:15 (30 minute periods with 5 minutes between classes).																						
12:50–1:25			5-A	5-C		5-C		5-A		5-H	5-A	5-C	5-C	5-A	5-H	4-TH	5-C	5-H			5-A	5-H	5-C
1:30–2:05			5-H			5-H		5-C	5-C		5-C		4-AY		5-A	4-AY	4-AM	5-A		5-C		5-A	5-H
2:05–2:40	4-AM	4-AY	4-TH			4-TH	4-AY		4-AM	4-AY	4-AM	4-TH	4-AM	4-TH		4-AM	4-AY	4-TH		4-AM		4-TH	4-AY
2:45–3:45	Afternoon Announcements, Car-rider Dismissal (2:50–2:58); Buses Depart at 3:00																						

A = Art; C = Computers; G = Guidance; L = Library; M = Music; PE = Physical Education

Franklin County Public Schools Comprehensive School Improvement Plan

School: Boones Mill Elementary **Year:** 2001–2002

Goal 1: To improve student performance in language arts as measured by performance on local, state, and national assessments.

MEASURABLE OBJECTIVES	SPECIFIC ACTIVITIES	WHO IS RESPONSIBLE	TARGET DATES	BUDGET	EVALUATION
Grade K: **As is:** 97% of kindergarten students scored a 2 on the Franklin County Reading Rubric in May 2001. **Desired state:** Maintain or increase 97% of kindergarten students scoring a 2 or higher on the Franklin County Reading Rubric by May 2002.	**Curriculum:** 1. Align and utilize State Resource Guides, SOL Blueprints, and the FCPS curriculum guide, English Standards of Learning Sample Scope and Sequence K-5, K-5 Pacing Guides to purposefully plan for instruction.	All Instructional Staff	Ongoing September 2001–May 2002		Lesson Plans, Pacing Guides, Curriculum, Alignment Forms
Grade 1: **As is:** 72% of first grade students scored a 3 or higher on the Franklin County Reading Rubric in May 2001. **Desired state:** At least 75% of first grade students will score a 3 or higher on the Franklin County Reading Rubric by May 2002.	**Staff Development:** 2. Attend and implement strategies from the following professional development activities: • FCPS Word Study Workshops • PALS Training • Jean Blades Whole Body Learning In-Service • Marilyn Burns Math Training • Guided Reading • Instructional Technology Training	All Instructional Staff, Principal 1st–3rd Teachers All Instructional Staff, Principal 1st–2nd Teachers All Instructional Staff, Principal	Fall 2001 September 12, 2001 August 20, 2001 August 21, 2001 September 27, 2001 Ongoing September 2001–May 2002		Attendance Log of each session & Workshop Feedback from participants

(continued)

MEASURABLE OBJECTIVES	SPECIFIC ACTIVITIES	WHO IS RESPONSIBLE	TARGET DATES	BUDGET	EVALUATION
Grade 2: **As is:** 90% of second grade students passed (80% or more correct) the Franklin County Second Grade Reading Test when first administered in May 2001. **Desired state:** Maintain or increase 90% of second grade students passing (80% or greater) on the Franklin County Second Grade Reading Test when first administered in May 2002.	3. Develop, implement, and evaluate Personal Enhancement Plans (PEP2) in grade-level teams to improve instruction/student achievement through specific staff development opportunities as needs are identified by grade-level teams. The Master Instructional Schedule allows for weekly team collaborative planning time to facilitate on-going, job-embedded staff development.	All Instructional Staff, Principal	September 2001–May 2002 (Mid-year checkpoint)	$1,250.00	PEP Mid- and End-of-Year Evaluation
Grade 3: **As is:** Third graders scored a mean scaled score of 36 in the area of "plan, compose, and revise paragraphs, stories, letters, and reports" on the SOL Writing Subtest in May 2001. **Desired state:** Third graders will score a mean scaled score of 38 or greater in the area of "plan, compose, and revise paragraphs, stories, letters, and reports" on the SOL Writing Subtest in May 2002.	**Instruction:** 4. Create/implement a master instructional schedule to provide protected blocks of instructional time; daily "specials" classes for all students; individual planning time for all instructional staff; and weekly collaborative planning for all instructional staff. Utilize support staff for supervision of students during cultural arts assemblies to allow for monthly cross-grade team collaboration.	All Instructional Staff, Principal	August 2001–June 2002		Results of Faculty Survey –January 2001 & June 2002
	5. Initiate individual/small group programs for additional learning time for students who have not met the targeted grade level benchmarks for identified SOL skills.	Teachers, Tutors, Parent Volunteers, RIS Coordinator	September 2001–May 2002		Volunteer Log in Office, Tutorial Schedule, Lesson Plans

(continued)

MEASURABLE OBJECTIVES	SPECIFIC ACTIVITIES	WHO IS RESPONSIBLE	TARGET DATES	BUDGET	EVALUATION
Grade 4: **As is:** 33% of fourth graders scored 78% or greater on the 9 FCPS Reading Rubric Subtests in May 2001. **Desired state:** At least 50% of fourth graders will score 78% or greater on the 9 FCPS Reading Rubric Subtests in May 2002.	6. Utilize Accelerated Reader software and monitor students' reading level, percent correct, and achievement of individual and classroom reading goals.	All Instructional Staff, Principal	September 2001–May 2002	$250.00	Accelerated Reader Reports
As is: The national percentile for fourth grade vocabulary on the Stanford 9 test was 57% in October 2000. **Desired state:** The national percentile for the fourth grade vocabulary on the Stanford 9 test will be 62% or greater in Oct. 2001.	7. Provide parents with resources and strategies to help their children succeed academically. Information will be provided on a regular basis through grade level workshops, classroom and school newsletters, and parent-teacher conferences.	All Instructional Staff, Principal	September 2001–May 2002		Workshop Attendance Logs, Study Guides, Newsletters, and Conference Logs
Grade 5: **As is:** Fifth graders scored a mean scaled score of 36 in the area of "understand a variety of printed materials/resource materials" on the SOL Reading/Literature and Research English Subtest in May 2001. **Desired state:** Fifth graders will score a mean scaled score of 37 or greater in the area of "understand a variety of printed materials/resource materials" on the SOL Reading/Literature and Research English Subtest in May 2002.	8. Utilize a variety of instructional strategies to target identified skills at each grade level. **Assessments:** 9. Develop and implement local common assessments (used by all teachers at each grade level) using standardized testing format with stem starters to provide students with multiple opportunities to respond to high-order questions.	All Instructional Staff, Principal Grade-level teams, Principal	September 2001–May 2002 September 2001–May 2002 (checkpoints at end-of-nine-weeks)		Lesson Plans, Classroom Observations, Team Feedback Sheets, & faculty meeting agendas Lesson Plans, Assessments, FC Reading Rubric K-5

(continued)

Franklin County Public Schools Comprehensive School Improvement Plan

School: Boones Mill Elementary   **Year:** 2001–2002

Goal 2: To improve student achievement in math as measured by performance on local, state, and national assessments.

MEASURABLE OBJECTIVES	SPECIFIC ACTIVITIES	WHO IS RESPONSIBLE	TARGET DATES	BUDGET	EVALUATION
Grade 3: **As is:** Third graders scored a mean scaled score of 37 in the area of "number and number sense" on the Math SOL test in May 2001. **Desired state:** Third graders will score a mean scaled score of 39 or greater in the area of "number and number sense" on the Math SOL test in May 2002.	**Curriculum:** 1. Align and utilize the following: State Resource Guides, SOL Blueprints, FCPS Curriculum Guide, Math Standards of Learning Sample Scope and Sequence K-5, K-5 locally developed Pacing Guides to plan for instruction.	All Instructional Staff	Ongoing September 2001–May 2002		Lesson Plans, Pacing Guides, Curriculum Alignment Forms
Grade 4: **As is:** 4% of the fourth grade students scored 70% or greater on the Flanagan Mott Math Pretest/Posttest in October 2001. **Desired state:** At least 80% of the fourth grade students will score 70% or greater on the Flanagan Mott Math Pretest/Posttest in May 2002.	**Staff Development:** 2. Attend and implement strategies from the following professional development activities: • Jean Blades Whole Body Learning In-Service • Marilyn Burns Math Training	All Instructional Staff, Principal	August 20, 2001 August 21, 2001		Attendance Logs & Workshop Feedback

(continued)

MEASURABLE OBJECTIVES	SPECIFIC ACTIVITIES	WHO IS RESPONSIBLE	TARGET DATES	BUDGET	EVALUATION
As is: The national percentile for fourth grade math procedures on the Stanford 9 was 53% in October 2000. **Desired state:** The national percentile for fourth grade math procedures will be 58% or greater in October 2001. **Grade 5:** **As is:** Fifth graders scored a mean scaled score of 34 in the area of measurement and geometry on the Math SOL test in May 2001. **Desired state:** Fifth graders will score a mean scaled score of 36 in the area of measurement and geometry on the Math SOL test in May 2002.	3. Develop, implement, and evaluate Personal Enhancement Plans (PEP2) in grade-level teams to improve instruction/student achievement through specific staff development opportunities as needs are identified by grade-level teams. The Master Instructional Schedule allows for weekly team collaborative planning time to facilitate ongoing, job-embedded staff development. **Instruction:** 4. Create/implement a master instructional schedule to provide protected blocks of instructional time; daily "specials" classes for all students; individual planning time and weekly collaborative planning for all instructional staff. Utilize support staff for supervision of students during cultural arts assemblies to allow for monthly cross-grade team collaboration. 5. Initiate individual and small group programs to provide additional learning time for students who have not met the targeted grade level benchmarks for identified SOL skills.	All Instructional Staff All Instructional Staff, Principal Teachers, Tutors, Volunteers, RIS Coordinator, Principal	September 2001–May 2002 August 2001–May 2002 September 2001–May 2002 (checkpoints at end-of-nine-weeks)	$1,250.00	PEP Mid- and End-of-Year Evaluations; Team Products; Faculty surveys—January & June Volunteer Log; Tutorial Schedule; Data Analysis Forms; Lesson Plans

(continued)

154

MEASURABLE OBJECTIVES	SPECIFIC ACTIVITIES	WHO IS RESPONSIBLE	TARGET DATES	BUDGET	EVALUATION
	6. Provide parents with resources and strategies to help their children succeed academically. Information will be provided on a regular basis through grade level workshops, classroom & school newsletters, and parent-teacher conferences.	All Instructional Staff, Principal	September 2001– May 2002		Number of Parents in Attendance, Study Guides & Newsletters
	7. Utilize flashcards, software, math centers, and manipulatives to deliver meaningful & varied instruction in math skills and content.	All Instructional Staff	August 2001– June 2002	$250.00	Lesson Plans & Classroom Observations
	8. Utilize Accelerated Math software to assist in providing individualized instruction and assessment.	3rd–5th Grades instructional Staff	August 2001– June 2002		Accelerated Math Reports
	Assessments: 9. Develop and implement local common assessments (used by all teachers at each grade level) using standardized testing format with stem starters to provide students with multiple opportunities to respond to high-order questions.	Grade-level teams, Principal	September 2001– May 2002		Lesson Plans, Assessments, Student Achievement Results

Quality Indicators Questionnaire for Successful School Improvement Planning

1. Was there widespread involvement in the development of the school improvement plan?

   - Were teachers involved?

   - Were parents involved?

   - Were community leaders involved?

   - If appropriate, were students involved?

2. Were processes used that led to consensus regarding the school improvement plan?

   - In developing the plan, was consensus reached regarding beliefs about the school's mission, the school's clientele, and teaching and learning?

   - How broad is the support for the plan?

   - Are key individuals and groups committed to implementing the plan?

3. Was an analysis of student performance data the primary focus of discussions about areas in which the school needed to improve?

   • Was student achievement data disaggregated or broken down into sub-areas so that plans could be developed to address specific, rather than broad, areas of concern.

4. When deciding on activities and initiatives to undertake in order to improve your school, was relevant research examined?

   • Are the activities and initiatives that will be undertaken as a part of the school improvement plan based primarily, but not exclusively, on the effective-schools research?

   • Were any survey instruments used to collect data about various aspects of effective schooling such as school climate or parent satisfaction?

5. Have specific improvement targets or goals been identified?

   • Are the goals attainable?

   • Are there adequate resources?

   • Have specific responsibilities been assigned?

   • Is there a timeline or target dates for the completion of activities or initiatives?

6. To what extent does the school improvement plan focus on teaching and learning?

- If all of the goals identified in the school improvement plan are obtained, what is the likelihood that student performance will be significantly impacted?

7. Is there a plan for monitoring the ongoing activities that were identified in the school improvement plan?

   - Who has the primary responsibility for monitoring the implementation of the plan?

   - What are the plans for keeping faculty and parents informed?

8. Have plans been developed to recognize and celebrate improvement that occurs?

Chapter 7

Case Studies

The following case studies illustrate how two school districts approached some of the cultural shifts necessary for becoming professional learning communities.

Supporting Schools as Professional Learning Communities: The District Context

By Patricia Taylor
Assistant Superintendant for Instruction
Frederick County Public Schools

Our school district might be viewed as transitional. Frederick County, Virginia, is located in the northern beginnings of the Shenandoah Valley. The orchards and agri-science industries that were once its mainstays are now sharing attention with the services and employment options that follow a growing population. The opportunities of Washington, DC, 60 miles to the east, have made Frederick County a desirable location for families who bring with them expanded expectations for their public schools.

New leaders are joining the district, and roles are evolving. This changing leadership requires re-teaching about a culture that has come to be characterized by collaborative decision-making, an administrative focus on instruction, purposeful instructional discussions at school and division levels, data sharing and analysis, attention to curriculum alignment, communication of academic expectations among all stakeholders, curriculum development linked to study of effective practices and programs, and improved student performance.

An important part of the Frederick County Public Schools story is about the reorganizing of central office resources to support its schools—first in practicing the processes of school improvement planning and then in transitioning to results-oriented professional learning communities. Over time, we have come to believe that sustained progress can be made when a district consciously focuses its central resources on supporting building-level performance improvement efforts.

How Did We Begin?

Nine years ago, our superintendent challenged the administrative team to move the district beyond the prevailing perception of "average and acceptable" and to seek to become an excellent school district as measured by a range of performance indicators. Our intent was to raise district-wide performance standards while we supported schools in their school improvement efforts, and we expected improvement to happen as a result of their planning efforts. We embraced the phrase "we monitor what we value" and asked ourselves hard questions about what we as district leaders had and had not been monitoring. The questions we chose to ask and the questions we avoided revealed much about our leadership. We sought an internal change in culture and accepted personal responsibilities for initiating, guiding, and sustaining that change.

We agreed that substantive change requires leadership at all levels, but that district-level leadership would need to model what was expected. District leaders would need to be willing to recreate systems, processes, and access to resources to invite participation at other levels. In some ways, inviting participation in this way might be viewed as elimination of excuses not to participate. We also agreed that change is incremental and takes place over time—but that evidence of positive change must be seen in the short term. The superintendent's repeated reminder to administrators and teachers was that change is a process, not an event. Sudden and dramatic student performance changes were not necessarily sought; instead high value was placed on gradual and continued improvements that avoided year-to-year fluctuations and explanations.

A year of training was initiated to assure principals' confidence in leading their school improvement teams and to build understanding among district-level administrators about their role in supporting principals. Following this training, we held a weeklong summer institute for core teams from each school. During the next year, schools collaboratively developed statements reflecting their mission, vision, and values and then developed plans that targeted specific improvements. The first years of planning were marked by a need to be more data-driven and to more accurately target efforts that would improve student achievement levels. The superintendent frequently shared his commitment to the concept of "teacher leader" and to the school improvement process during meetings and school visits. It was clear for a number of years that his affirmation was needed as administrators and teachers wondered if "this too shall pass." By year 6, school improvement and teachers' important role in school improvement had become part of our institutional culture.

District-Level Changes

While we stressed that the results that mattered were to be found at the school level, we recognized the essential role of district-level staff in helping schools to implement their improvement plans. In fact, we found that the central office role required as much attention as the role of school leaders. It was imperative that building administrators would find in us the models for the leadership we asked of them. We acknowledged that our personal responses to the changes asked of us would become a standard others would consider when faced with changes that would affect them. Leaders of instruction, transportation, human resources, building and grounds, technology, and finance departments participated in school improvement training with all other administrators and developed a sense of their role in bringing their department resources to bear on the improvement efforts of the individual schools. Gradually, we shared with principals much of what might be viewed as the elements of central office power—options over district schedules, staff development direction, funds for individual school's training needs, access among schools to each other's performance data, and increased participation in policy and program decisions. Funds were provided to principals to bring school planning teams together during noncontract time or to free teams to meet on contract days. We modified many long-standing practices and procedures that principals identified as interfering with school improvement efforts. Department leaders were encouraged to consider flexibility with administrative details when doing so would help a principal's efforts without violating requirements beyond our authority or creating program inequities for students.

Instructional Staff Commitments

The central instructional staff found several immediate ways to communicate its support of individual school improvement. In many ways, these efforts did not represent change as much as they represented improved focus that resulted in more effective use of the staff's resources by schools.

- Quality staff development experiences that focused on school improvement plan goals included seeking out the best available consultants and funding the development of excellent trainers within the district.

- District resources were shifted to assure principals increased funds to send staff to leadership and content-related conferences.

- Agendas for monthly instructional meetings with principals and district instructional staff shifted from information given by district staff to collaborative discussion of issues, sharing strategies, and problem-solving; before decisions that would impact all schools were finalized, each principal was asked to express the best option for his or her school.

- Instructional supervisors visited principals for private briefings on new curriculum documents to assure that principals understood these resources before beginning their teacher observation and conference cycles.

- Minutes from division curriculum team meetings were shared with principals and teachers in all schools to prompt communication and discussion about instructional issues and pending decisions.

- Instructional supervisors were included in all teacher interviews to team with principals in focusing on key instructional elements.

- Memos from division staff became less frequent, and more often reflected the direction that was collaboratively determined.

These changes in how the staff carried out their instructional leadership responsibilities were important, but equally important was a commitment by district instructional staff to these five guiding points as their particular contribution to support school improvement:

1. Actively share best practices research with school staff in order to build a common vocabulary and discussion points for school improvement teams.

2. Be attentive to data and initiate data collection where it has been lacking.

3. Refocus reliance on district-level leadership and initiatives for student performance improvement to school-level leadership and initiatives aligned to school data.

4. Avoid bandwagon approaches and professional jargon.

5. Learn to celebrate successes and to understand how and why they happened.

Share Best Practices Research

While instructional supervisors shared research with teachers during conferences, committee meetings, and workshops, discussion was promoted by three additional initiatives. First, a "teacher researcher" graduate class taught by one of the district's teachers was added to the annual schedule of staff development classes; the teacher, class members, a university representative, and the assistant superintendent for instruction collaboratively developed guidelines for teacher research in the district. Second, the local reading association collaborated with central instructional staff to arrange financial support and a license renewal incentive for staff involved in "teachers as readers" groups; the original group multiplied to 24 groups of teachers and administrators who select, read, and discuss together professional books and books of interest to their students. Third, content area lead teachers were established in each elementary and middle school; a counterpart to high school department heads, lead teachers are encouraged to communicate with each other and central instructional staff outside of scheduled meetings through an electronic discussion board established on the district server.

Be Attentive to Data

We agreed to use our growing technology resources to help us better understand our institutional strengths and needs. We realized that increased attention to data would require helping our schools face the sensitive issue of sharing individual school performance data much more openly than had been the practice—among schools and with the community. We focused on identifying effective programs and practices and providing information to principals and teachers from which they could gain perspective on their specific efforts. We successfully sought the addition of a district-level staff position—coordinator of assessment and program evaluation. While this person's role included the management of testing programs, the more important responsibility was helping schools to gather and analyze meaningful data and to evaluate the effectiveness of their programs and initiatives in improving student performance. Principals were asked to analyze data, but the central staff was responsible for assuring that data were available and efficiently retrievable. Today, many data formats are provided to schools that can be easily reconfigured, and on-site analysis assistance is easily available to teachers and principals.

Focus on School-based Leadership

As principals were charged with an expanded leadership role including development of school improvement teams with wide representation, district-level departments began to view themselves as support teams for principals. The central instructional staff found that principals who had communicated neutral positions toward curriculum efforts and training became more interested, supportive, and even proactive regarding this work. Curriculum improvement teams comprised of representative teachers from each school were initiated for each content area. Teachers serving on these teams were designated as liaisons between the team and the teachers in their schools. We stressed that curriculum was developed centrally, but that implementation was a school responsibility. As confidence in this shared responsibility grew, principals began to lead curriculum alignment projects at their schools, seeking assistance from central staff and outside consultants. Curriculum development and alignment efforts initiated more interest in who was and was not learning what was expected. As we explored criterion-referenced testing projects, a measure of anxiety was being created by the development of a state testing program based on content standards and linked to graduation requirements and individual school accreditation status. The upside of this anxiety was the focusing of teacher attention on the importance of test construction, the potential value of criterion-referenced test data, and public interest in quantifiable measures of student learning. Carefully chosen or developed district-wide assessments are now imbedded with required state tests, and individual schools determine other assessments that are needed to monitor who is and who is not learning what is expected.

Avoid Bandwagons and Jargon

Choosing not to pursue one of the many business improvement models of the decade, we turned to the effective schools research of our profession. We agreed to keep our school improvement plan model simple, to link state and district initiatives to school plans when possible, and to eliminate redundant processes. We chose to avoid vocabulary understandable only to an inner circle—especially when that inner circle excluded parents. A continuing effort aims to improve communication among educators, students, parents, and other patrons by explaining terms and then substituting the definition for the term when possible. For example, we ask district staff's thoughtful consideration before including new and undefined terminology in curriculum documents or training programs. This staff also provides leadership in identifying programs or products with potential long-term merit and programs with probable short-term attractiveness.

Celebrate and Understand Success

Understanding the difference between "bragging" and affirming the results of intentional efforts was important for leaders, especially within a school district whose culture valued professional modesty. Instructional supervisors focused on the classroom as the most important place for monitoring success and embraced a supervisory coaching model that prompts teachers to identify their classroom successes, to consider the "why" behind those successes, and to share their understandings with other professionals. While classroom successes were the heart of our work, each school and department annually listed what it believed to be its best successes and submitted them to the assistant superintendent for instruction. These successes continue to be shared during the summer months over our district's cable television channel, submitted to the county government administrator for his information, and spotlighted in a special video production shown at the annual pre-school staff convocation.

Leadership Transition: Merging School Improvement Processes, Results Orientation, and Professional Learning Community Qualities

Many school divisions experience the end of a culture when a change in superintendent occurs. Seven years into our effort, that might have happened to us—but it didn't. We would like to believe that the foundation of communication, expectation, and recognition of successes was an inviting agenda to our new superintendent. Following an intensive interview with each district-level department head and principal during which challenges and results were explored, the superintendent affirmed the worth of our efforts and invited those leaders to focus with him on the next level—becoming a professional learning community. He noted that, as we improved our skills in planning and monitoring our improvement efforts, we were preparing to deepen the cultural change that was underway. Our beginning efforts had focused on monitoring data and considering questions we asked and questions we avoided, but, over time, we had moved toward emphasizing the importance of professional conversations and study groups. While in many ways we already had moved toward becoming a professional learning community, we also faced several immediate challenges:

1. Scheduled retirements within several years of nearly half the principals, assistant principals, and district-level administrators required detailed attention to culture and process.

2. Documents that served as road maps for processes would be needed to guide new administrators.

3. Results orientation had become more critical than when the division's improvement efforts were initiated 7 years earlier, and principals needed assistance in helping staff to become more results-oriented without becoming discouraged.

4. Focus on professional conversation had become increasingly important as a means of planning for and monitoring results.

Response to the Challenges

During the new superintendent's first year, he focused attention on reviewing basic school improvement planning concepts, reducing fears related to state test data monitoring, and acknowledging incremental gains toward stated goals. Monthly administrative meetings included agenda time for discussion of readings on those topics. The superintendent's school visits and conferences with principals included conversations about their school improvement plan goals. At the annual administrative summer session, the consultant who had assisted the division 8 years earlier joined the superintendent in linking our efforts to date with the foundation elements of a professional learning community. At that session, principals helped design one of the needed guiding documents for new administrators—a month-by-month chart of the school improvement process.

Instructional supervisors implemented an instructional coaching approach focused on initiating professional conversations about the teaching process—planning, teaching, and reflecting. As an outgrowth of their conversations with teachers, they developed a professional discussion guide intended to help other administrators initiate similar conversations, but it became clear that the guide had a much wider application in a professional learning community. The printed guide was placed in the hands of every teacher and administrator as a tool for helping everyone focus on the important questions about instruction from our perspectives of teacher, mentor, department head, lead teacher, student teacher, supervisor, and administrator. A videotape demonstrated use of the guide's questions, each faculty member was trained on the intent and use of the guide, and all were invited into the process of professional conversation.

A current project is to design into the administrative evaluation process the opportunity to reflect on leadership expectations in a professional learning community that is focused on incremental school improvement. It acknowledges to our administrators that we value and expect the leadership that is required to build a results orientation in our schools and to do so through shared leadership approaches that invite the ideas of all stakeholders.

Lessons Learned

Two very important points arose from the many lessons affirmed during our school improvement efforts. First, change occurs over time. We must balance between patience and impatience to assure that we are pursuing incremental gains that lead to improvements in student achievement. Second, if school division leaders hope to inspire their schools to become professional learning communities, they must be prepared to provide very specific supports to the school leaders. Some of those supports require tangible resources; some supports require that we demonstrate what we are seeking through our own leadership behaviors.

In school improvement leadership, we believe that the potential for substantive change resides at the school among the professionals and others who care about the schools' students. However, we also believe that the central services of a school district exist to be of significant support to its schools in that effort. As our current superintendent reminds *all employees,* there is only one reason for each of us to come to work each day, and that is to do our part to make our students successful in learning the content and skills determined to be important for them to master. That reminder renews our focus and energy, and, when appropriate, our patience with goals set too far into the future to help children who need our best efforts now.

We began with training and support of our school leaders in school improvement efforts and then focused on development of a district-wide plan for improvement. We asked ourselves what it was that we wanted our students to learn and whether or not our students were learning what it was we established as important. While focusing on instruction and assessment of student learning, it also became important to reflect on our own leadership efforts and to assure that they were aligned with our beliefs about school improvement. Our continuing challenge is to assure that the culture of collaborative decision-making, school improvement, results-orientation, and professional conversation at all levels has the opportunity to continue. The beliefs and practices that make up our culture must be lived and talked about if they are to be sustained and improved upon by the leaders who will follow us.

Aligning Effort:
What Do We Want Students to Learn?

By Mary Ann Ranells
Deputy Superintendent of Public Instruction
Idaho Department of Education

In the late 1980s, Twin Falls was known as a good school district, but staff members were dissatisfied with the status quo. Turnover in top administrative positions had become commonplace, teachers were working hard but found the isolation stifling, and a sense of disconnectedness was growing. The journey toward professional learning community status began with the hiring of a new superintendent in 1990 by a board of trustees anxious to support staff in moving the district forward. It all began when the chairman of the board spoke to the administrative team. He told a powerful story of his early experiences in school as a nonreader, what he had to do to survive, and what happened when a teacher took him aside and helped him acquire the tools necessary to become a lifelong learner. He experienced many successes and setbacks before earning a doctorate. With that story, the vision was set, and now our greatest responsibility is to be sure there is a teacher in every classroom who cares that every student learns and grows.

---

*Dr. Ranells is the former Director of Curriculum and Instruction, Twin Falls School District #411, Twin Falls, Idaho.

Building a Capacity for Change

With the support of the board and superintendent, the staff experienced a renewed commitment to providing a quality education to all children. During the 1990s, the district focused on building a capacity for change. Teams of teachers and administrators began reading research, attending national conferences on school improvement, and visiting schools around the country in search of a quality improvement model. Community members were invited to assist in the development of a mission statement and strategic plan. An ongoing dialog captured the values and beliefs of who we wanted to become and how we would treat one another in the process. Empowerment, professionalism, constancy of purpose, kindness, and determination were identified as crucial behaviors. Teaming became the single most important element as we worked internally and externally to build the capacity for change. Every person had an important role in our successes.

Designing a Governance Structure

In 1992, the district adopted a belief system, articulated an achievement model, and designed a governance structure. The Quality School Committee (QSC) was formed as the primary vehicle for providing the leadership necessary to design, implement, and evaluate program improvements. Membership included teacher, administrator, and parent representatives from every school. They met six times a year and served as the governing body for all school improvement initiatives. This group strongly believed that all students could learn and that expectations needed to increase. They believed that identifiable, obtainable, and rigorous outcomes were essential in an improvement model. They believed that governance must be accessible to all. Input came to QSC through individual teachers, grade-level teams, parents, and subject-area committees. Three important subcommittees grew out of the QSC—the Curriculum Committee, the

Instruction Committee, and the Communication Committee—which began the detailed work necessary to achieve the goals.

Building a Commitment to Accountability

It took time, courageous patience, and constant communication to build a strong foundation based on shared beliefs, research, and best practice. Through the tremendous efforts of the staff, what was once just a vision for the future gradually took firm root in reality. William Glasser trained the staff in Control Theory and his work became the philosophical underpinnings of the district. After visiting several sites of excellence, the QSC adopted the Outcome Driven Developmental Model (ODDM) as the process the district would use as its anchor to design a system of high academic accountability. John Champlain, Jake Burks, and educators from various districts came to Twin Falls to train staff on the process known as The Success Connection. This process required staff to answer four seemingly innocent questions: What do you want? What do you believe about what you want? What do you know about what you want in terms of research and best practice? What will you do to get what you want? After much discussion and investigation, the staff made a bold commitment to the following goals:

- Develop K-12 curriculums in all subject areas that will clearly outline what students should know and be able to do.

- Embrace those instructional strategies that will yield the highest academic gain.

- Design an assessment system to determine if students have learned what was taught.

- Focus on a reporting system to clearly communicate to students and parents each child's progress in relation to expected outcomes.

The ODDM Wars

During the 1993-94 school year, the ODDM Wars, as they are affectionately called, rocked the district and community. The confusion, mistrust, and misunderstanding of outcome-based education created such havoc and discontent within the district and community that it was feared all was lost. Instead of giving up, instead of running for cover, instead of firing the top administrators, the Board of Trustees stood firm. The staff stood firm. The administrators stood firm. They believed so strongly in what they were doing that they went out into the community and met with civic organizations, business leaders, government officials, and parents to share their vision of providing the quality education necessary for students to succeed in life. The good people of Twin Falls liked what they heard, or at least adopted a "wait and see" attitude. The resistance subsided enough to allow staff to refocus their energies on the goals.

Focusing on Instruction

In 1994, The Quality School Committee selected a number of teachers and administrators to become trainers in Control Theory/Responsibility Training, Cooperative Learning, Mastery Learning, ODDM, and Learning Styles. Three days of training during each summer and four days during the school year provided all staff members with the opportunity to learn and implement best instructional practices. We have been fortunate to learn from some of the country's top experts, but our best sessions for staff development have been when our teachers and administrators provided the training— we just had to get to the point where we wanted to do it ourselves.

As teachers and administrators acquired new knowledge, they began developing an instructional model to guide their craft. It was also during this time that the Classroom Practices Booklet was initiated. This booklet provided the guidelines for excellence in teaching. Topics covered in the booklet included inclusion, grading, attendance, correctives, extensions, discipline, testing, and home-work. As each practice was being developed, members of the QSC sought input from each faculty member before the final approval was granted. The Classroom Practices Booklet and the instructional model have since become living documents in the district, and the staff development programs have become institutionalized.

Developing Standards and Assessments

Beginning in 1995, the district contracted with the Mid-continent Regional Educational Laboratory to convert curriculum guides in the core subjects into standards-based documents. As committees of teachers reviewed and revised the standards and benchmarks, they also developed summative assessments for each grade level in math, science, language arts, and social studies. This process involved front-loading benchmarks and objectives based on teacher expertise as well as back-loading skills, concepts, processes, and ideas assessed on state-mandated tests.

We began this chapter of our story by bringing together district-wide committees of teachers. For example, meeting as a district-wide K–12 language arts committee, representative teachers from each grade level identified K–12 standards, interval grade level bench-marks, and specific grade-level objectives. The committee carefully analyzed the seven standards they felt would best ensure student suc-cess. Based on each standard, they wrote benchmarks for the end of grades three, six, nine, and twelve that would serve as interval targets for success as students moved up through the system. Next, the twelfth grade English teachers answered two questions. First, "What can we guarantee our students will learn as a result of our instruction to help them achieve the twelfth grade benchmarks?" For each stan-dard and benchmark they identified grade-level objectives they felt would be required for student mastery. For each objective, they dis-cussed how they would assess the objective. If they agreed an objective was not necessary for mastery, they abandoned it. The second question was, "What do we wish students would know and be able to do when they come to us from their junior year?" Then the eleventh grade teachers took the twelfth grade English "wish list" and designed their grade-level objectives and assessment ideas to meet the benchmark. This "design down" process continued through the grade levels to kindergarten.

It soon became painfully clear that we could not teach it all. Identifying the "have-to-knows" versus the "nice-to-knows" helped focus the curriculum on what was truly important in terms of student mastery. This was achieved in large part by developing the summative (end-of-year) assessments as we wrote the standards, benchmarks, and grade-level objectives. Organized abandonment was, and still is, one of our greatest challenges. Giving up a favorite unit, learning how to spiral the "have-to-knows" throughout the year, and implementing an accountability system was both exhilarating and frightening.

As of 2000, summative assessments (including a K–12 Direct Writing Assessment) have been developed and administered in all core and elective areas. This process has contributed to accomplishing coordination within a grade level and articulation across all grade levels. Focus on student achievement weighs much heavier now than when we merely "tried to cover it all."

Cycle for Assessment, Analysis, and Action

From 1996–1999, as teachers began compiling data from the summative assessments and analyzing the data in relation to state testing data, strengths and weaknesses were defined, improvement goals were written, and action plans were implemented to close the gap between what students knew versus what they did not know. The annual cycle for assessment, analysis, and action included a number of steps:

1. Each spring, teachers administered, scored, and compiled summative assessment data by subject and grade level.

2. Grade level teams in each building compiled results, identified patterns, analyzed and interpreted the patterns, and determined improvement goals for the next academic year.

3. Each faculty met to hear grade-level team report findings, conclusions, and goals.

4. Each faculty identified patterns and trends and set building improvement goals. Buildings reported their results and goals to the QSC, and the QSC identified district-wide improvement goals.

5. Teachers met district-wide by grade level to analyze district data in terms of curriculum coordination.

6. Teachers met across grade levels to examine patterns and trends in terms of curriculum articulation. The Board of Trustees and the Twin Falls Education Association negotiated two additional contract days to allow teachers additional time for data analysis and goal setting.

Designing a Better Reporting System

In 1997, based on the alignment of the written, taught, and tested curriculum, elementary teachers designed a new report card to provide students and parents with more in-depth information regarding student performance in relation to the content standards.

For example, instead of a single letter grade for math, sixth grade students and parents also receive feedback on how the students are doing on place value, fractions, decimals, estimation, problem solving, measurement, geometry, and statistics. With additional information, teachers and parents are better able to assist students with specific areas of difficulty. Students are more aware of and feel more accountable for their own learning. As students progress from grade level to grade level, they are beginning to see that what they learn at one level actually has something to do with their success at the next. They can see the connection, possibly for the first time, and feel some confidence that the targets will remain stable. When the teachers provide feedback to the students, they are now able to indicate which standards are being met and which still need some work.

Developing Intervention Strategies

Once the district decided to focus on student achievement, it became clear that we would need to provide assistance to students who did not learn what we had planned for them to learn. After reviewing the research and literature on retention and social promotion and finding little or no evidence that these options worked, we decided to pilot intervention strategies such as extended-day tutoring programs, summer school, and direct instruction in small group settings. While we are still analyzing the strengths and weaknesses of various models of intervention, this appears to be one of the most important components of our school improvement efforts to date.

Renewing and Recommitting

In 1997, we decided to update the Strategic Plan. During the school year, five separate community focus groups were convened to review the first strategic plan—what had been accomplished and what still needed to be done. These focus groups consisted of broad community representation—business, government, religion, higher education, senior citizens, etc. The following year we met with five employee focus groups and adhered to the same process. Membership on the employee focus groups included teachers, students, administrators, teacher assistants, secretaries, custodians, and food service employees. Once a draft document was written, all participants in the focus groups received a copy for review. A final work session was held to revise and finalize the document. The new

Strategic Plan was then presented to the Quality School Committee. QSC members presented it to each building staff for review before endorsement and Board of Trustee approval. Once again we learned the document was secondary in importance to the 2-year process of involving all stakeholders in a meaningful dialogue regarding the future of the district. Our Strategic Plan focused on the following key areas:

1. Increase accountability for student learning and achievement.

2. Establish a rigorous curriculum based on clearly stated learning standards.

3. Expand learning opportunities to better meet the educational needs of all students.

4. Improve communication with the community and employees.

5. Involve parents and the community in district activities and decision-making.

6. Ensure a safe, secure, and caring learning environment.

7. Reinforce the citizenship skills necessary to function as a contributing member of society.

Amazingly, these goals are very similar to the first strategic plan. The message from our stakeholders seemed very clear—"Stay the course."

Results

Based on all the data available from ITBS/TAP, Direct Writing Assessment, Direct Math Assessment, SAT, ACT, district summative assessments, Wateford, grades, and other classroom sources, it appears district efforts to increase student achievement are paying off. Overall district comparison of just the ITSB/TAP results from 1995 compared to 1999 reveal significant growth. One school boasted composite scores in the 92nd percentile in grades 3, 4, and 5, with sixth grade at the 84th percentile in 1999. Another elementary school achieved a 40% gain on the subtest for Written Expression. In tracking this year's sixth graders in mathematics, the data reveals continuous growth. As third graders, these students scored in the 56th percentile in 1996; in 1997 as fourth graders, they scored in the 68th percentile; in the fifth grade they scored at the 71st percentile; and this year as sixth graders they scored at the 86th percentile. Our alternative high school students have gone from 38% passing the eleventh grade Direct Writing Assessment to 88% passing in 1999. The number of sixth grade students eligible for seventh grade advanced math has more than doubled. Reading achievement at our primary level is the highest compared to nine other large school districts in the state.

Lessons Learned

The journey of providing a quality education to every child is not an easy one. We continue to have great debates over issues that challenge our old belief system. What we are doing is not innovative or glitzy. It's just hard, often tedious work. It is often difficult to keep our focus. There always seems to be someone or something out there promising to have the magic cure. We are tempted to jump on yet another bandwagon, but we know that is the wrong thing to do. We haven't been awarded big dollars from any grant or foundation to do this. Funding is never enough to do the job. Twin Falls ranks 100 out of 112 school districts in per pupil expenditures. We have 27 languages spoken in our schools, 40% of students are on free or reduced lunch, and parental involvement (or the perceived lack thereof) is a significant issue. Communication continues to be a challenge and often hinders our work together. Yet through all this, our mentors have taught us to persist, to be stubborn, and to keep the target steady. Our students are demonstrating higher academic achievement. That's what we wanted. That's what we are getting. That's what we will continue to do.

Bibliography

Bennis, W., & Nanus, B. (1985). *Leaders: The strategies for taking charge.* New York: Harper and Row.

Covey, S. (1989). *The seven habits of highly effective people: Restoring the character ethic.* New York: Franklin Press.

Drucker, P. (1992). Managing for the future: The 1990s and beyond. New York: Truman Talley Books.

Drucker, P. (1996). Not enough generals were killed. In F. Hesselbein, M. Goldsmith, & R. Beckhard (Eds.), *The leader of the future* (pp. xi-xv). San Francisco: Jossey-Bass.

DuFour, R. (1997a). Make the words of mission statements come to life. *Journal of Staff Development, 18*(3), 54–55.

DuFour, R. (1997b). Moving toward the school as a learning community. *Journal of Staff Development, 18*(1), 52–53.

DuFour, R. (1997c). Seeing with new eyes. *Journal of Staff Development, 18*(4), 52–53.

DuFour, R., & Eaker, R. (1998). *Professional learning communities at work: Best practices for enhancing student achievement.* Bloomington, IN: National Educational Service.

Frankl, V. (1959*). Man's search for meaning.* New York: Pocket Books.

Greenleaf, R. (1982). *Servant as leader.* Indianapolis, IN: Robert Greenleaf Center for Servant Leadership.

James, J. (1996, December). Thinking in the future tense. Keynote address presented at the annual conference of the National Staff Development Council, Vancouver, BC.

Kotter, J. (1996). *Leading change.* Boston: Harvard Business School Press.

Sarason, S. (1996). *Revisiting the culture of the school and the problem of change.* New York: Teachers College Press.

Schmoker, M. (1996). *Results: The key to continuous school improvement.* Alexandria, VA: Association for Supervision and Curriculum Development.

About *Getting Started: Reculturing Schools to Become Professional Learning Communities* and the National Educational Service

The mission of the National Educational Service is to provide tested and proven resources that help those who work with youth create safe and caring schools, agencies, and communities where all children succeed. *Getting Started: Reculturing Schools to Become Professional Learning Communities* is just one of many resources and staff development opportunities NES provides that focus on building a community circle of caring. If you have any questions, comments, or manuscripts you would like us to consider for publication, please contact us at the address below or visit our website at:

www.nesonline.com

Staff Development Opportunities Include:

Bullying Prevention
Effective Parenting
Creating Professional Learning Communities
Building Cultural Bridges
Discipline With Dignity
Ensuring Safe Schools
Managing Disruptive Behavior
Reclaiming Youth at Risk
Teaching Self Control

National Educational Service
304 W. Kirkwood Avenue, Suite 2
Bloomington, IN 47404-5132
(812) 336-7700
(800) 733-6786 (toll-free number)
FAX (812) 336-7790
e-mail: nes@nesonline.com
www.nesonline.com

NEED MORE COPIES OR ADDITIONAL
RESOURCES ON THIS TOPIC?

Need more copies of this book? Want your own copy? Need additional resources on this topic? If so, you can order additional materials by using this form or by calling us toll free at (800) 733-6786 or (812) 336-7700. Or you can order by FAX at (812) 336-7790, or visit our website at www.nesonline.com.

Title	Price*	Quantity	Total
Getting Started: Reculturing Schools to Become Professional Learning Communities	$19.95		
Professional Learning Communities at Work (video set)	495.00		
Professional Learning Communities at Work (book)	24.95		
Cooperative Classroom	19.95		
Creating Learning Communities: The Role of the Teacher in the 21st Century	18.95		
Creating the New American School	21.95		
EdMarketing: How Smart Schools Get and Keep Community Support	24.95		
How to Create Alternative, Magnet, and Charter Schools	24.95		
Leading Schools to Quality (video and leader's guide)	250.00		
Reconnecting Youth: A Peer Group Approach to Building Life Skills	179.00		
		SUBTOTAL	
		SHIPPING	
Continental U.S.: Please add 6% of order total. Outside continental U.S.: Please add 8% of order total.			
		HANDLING	
Continental U.S.: Please add $4. Outside continental U.S.: Please add $6.			
		TOTAL (U.S. funds)	

*Price subject to change without notice.

❏ Check enclosed ❏ Purchase order enclosed
❏ Money order ❏ VISA, MasterCard, Discover, or American Express (circle one)

Credit Card No._____ Exp. Date_____
Cardholder Signature _____

SHIP TO:
First Name_____ Last Name _____
Position _____
Institution Name_____
Address_____
City_____ State_____ ZIP_____
Phone_____ FAX_____
E-mail _____

National Educational Service
304 W. Kirkwood Avenue, Suite 2
Bloomington, IN 47404-5132
(812) 336-7700 • (800) 733-6786 (toll-free number)
FAX (812) 336-7790
e-mail: nes@nesonline.com • www.nesonline.com